# Taking Time To Act

D1297802

# Taking Time To Act

## A GUIDE TO CROSS-CURRICULAR DRAMA

### Chris Ball
### John Airs

HEINEMANN • PORTSMOUTH, NEW HAMPSHIRE

Heinemann
A division of Reed Elsevier Inc.
361 Hanover Street
Portsmouth, NH 03801-3912

*Offices and agents throughout the world*

Cartoons by Bill Stott.

**Library of Congress Cataloging-in-Publication Data**

Ball, Chris.
    Taking time to act : a guide to cross-curricular drama / Chris Ball, John Airs.
      p.  cm.
    Includes bibliographical references.
    ISBN 0-435-08666-9 (pbk.)
    1. Drama in education.   I. Ball, Christopher, 1935–
II. Title.
    PN3171.A35   1995
371.3'32—dc20
                                  94-43586
                                      CIP

Editor: Lisa A. Barnett
Production: Camden Type 'n Graphics
Cover design: Phillip Augusta

Printed in the United States of America on acid-free paper
98  97  96  95     EB     1  2  3  4  5  6

# Contents

# A Foreword

FROM

## Willy Russell

author of *Educating Rita*, *Shirley Valentine*, *Blood Brothers*

I really found this to be an engaging and stimulating piece of work, so much so that it almost made me want to start teaching again!

I think one of the real pluses of it is that you have struck exactly the right tone; it is assured, confident, and informative, whilst still being written in an accessible and good natured language, authoritative without in any way being esoteric. Terrific.

Yours sincerely
WILLY

# Acknowledgments

Special thanks to Mersey Television, North West Arts Board,
and Liverpool TVE for funding help and support in producing the
original document that led to this publication.

T H A N K S   A L S O   T O

Alderwood Junior High School
Diane Auton
Pat Belvisi
Patricia Bishop
Waltraud Boxall
Janet Burns
Frank Dunn
First Bite Theatre Company
Peter Gibbons
Jean Gilbert
Jim Heaton
Pat Hughes
Robert Jeffcoate

Clive Lawton
Liverpool City Libraries
Derek Massey
Jackie Mcgrath
Pleasant Street J.M.I. School
Rejects Revenge Theatre Company
Roscoe Infants School
Willy and Annie Russell
St. Paschal Baylon J.M.I. School
Mike Shankland
Irene Travis
Polly Winn

A N D

All the students, parents and teachers we have
worked with over the last seven years

T H A N K S

Chris Ball
John Airs

# DRAMA IN EDUCATION
# What Is It?

## PLAY

Children learn through play; it helps them make sense of their experiences. Drama, at its simplest, is structured play. As we get older we tend to forget how to play. We pay others to do it for us. For some of us being a shepherd or (if we were really lucky) the Virgin Mary is just about the only memory we have of dramatic playing. If that is the case, we've missed out on a lot.

> Every child is an artist.
> The problem is how to remain an artist when he grows up.
>
> PABLO PICASSO

## MAKING SENSE OF THE WORLD

From the beginning of history, Drama has had the specific function in a society of both celebrating and challenging the values of that society. As with other Arts, but perhaps more obviously so, Drama is a way of making sense of the world.

It is not simply a matter of making sense by accommodating the world as it is now. It involves questioning it and seeing how it can be improved. What part can we play in shaping it? What parts are we responsible for? Moreover, it is a social activity that we undertake together.

1

> Theatre has the potential . . . of replacing a single viewpoint
> by a multitude of different visions.
>
> PETER BROOK

## DRAMA AND THE CURRICULUM

When we do Drama, we are employing a medium that children relish and are good at. Drama offers a context and a powerful motivation for learning. It promotes confidence and independence in the learners and it can permeate the whole curriculum. In spite of its omission as a foundation subject Drama permeates several of the core and foundation subjects of the national curriculum.

In the United States, Drama is being made mandatory in an increasing number of states. Some of its popularity may be attributed to an enthusiasm among educators and legislators for Howard Gardner's aim of designing and implementing "an education that yields understanding" and that "takes seriously the ideas and intuitions" of children, with their different kinds of intelligence and different ways of learning. It is not difficult to see how Drama, with its highly contextualized, student-centered approach to learning, opens several if not all of Gardner's "doors" onto most topics (see *The Unschooled Mind* [1991], page 244 and passim).

DRAMA IS A WAY TO TEACH ORIENTEERING, GEOGRAPHY, COMMUNICATIONS, AND PERSONAL AND SOCIAL EDUCATION.

In England and Wales, it is a statutory requirement for all children up to the age of fourteen. It is part of the English orders for the national curriculum and is referred to in the orders and guidelines for several other subjects. The influential *Cox Report, English 5–11* (1989), states:

> We see Drama as central to developing all major aspects of English in the primary school.

and

> Drama is of crucial importance as a learning medium.

> The nonstatutory guidance for History says:

> Drama can help pupils meet all History attainment targets.

The place of Drama as cross-curricular teaching methodology can be clearly established even within the confines of a national curriculum. The cross-curricular skills of oracy, listening, and communication are utilized in all Drama lessons. Drama is a basic. So let's get back to it!

## DRAMA AS A BASIC

Drama is an educational basic, but we must always bear in mind that it is an artistic and cultural basic as well. Within Drama, both Education and Art work in tandem. The British Arts Council in its document, *Towards a National Arts and Media Strategy* (1992), stresses that "the development of a cultural identity is a basic human need. . . . The Arts are central to this. . . . Those who are denied Arts opportunities are indeed deprived."

## DRAMA OR THEATRE?

> The unexamined life is not worth living.
>
> SOCRATES

Theatre is an art for examining life and examining it from many angles. Drama in Education is a form of theatre practice. We learn together through play making. We forge what we want to say in this workshop, this forum, in this theatre that is the classroom, and we develop the theatre skills, the Drama techniques to do it, whether we go on to perform it to an audience of others or not. Augusto Boal, whose work with adults has been adapted by many teachers to inform their practice, talks about "forms of a rehearsal theatre and not a spectacle theatre. One knows how these experiments will begin but not how they will end." Classroom Drama is this sort of theatre, an experimental exploratory theatre, whose actors are forging a vision for themselves, using all the resources of the art of theatre. The great beauty of this

3

form of theatre is that it can genuinely belong to the participants. It is their theatre. Our pupils learn through Drama and develop as artists in this most ordinary and extraordinary of art forms.

Drama in Education is a legitimate form of theatre. Our children are entitled to the experience of it. As teachers we can provide it. The joy and learning it offers are worth cherishing in our schools, perhaps more so now than ever before.

# Act One

# DRAMA IN SCHOOL
## The Stage You're At

### THINKING ABOUT IT

Every teacher is aware of

- children's entitlement to Drama
- educational possibilities of Drama
- statutory requirements for Drama

## TRYING THINGS OUT

Every teacher in the school is willing at least to try to include some drama techniques in her or his teaching program.

## FULLY COMMITTED

Whole-school approaches to active learning and to drama have been adopted as a matter of policy and practice. Drama has a place in every classroom, just like reading and writing.

DRAMA HAS A PLACE IN EVERY CLASSROOM, JUST AS DO READING AND
WRITING.

# Act Two

# TEACHER'S TOOL KIT

## AIM

The aim of this Teacher's Tool Kit is to encourage all teachers in every phase of education to use drama as a way of teaching across the curriculum.

The techniques and ideas that follow illustrate the ways in which the art of Drama can provide a stimulus and context for learning.

In terms of planning, starting, and managing a drama there are a number of practical questions that concern people. On the following pages, we suggest ways of dealing with them. No suggestions can be all-embracing, nor are the points raised necessarily always appropriate to every lesson. The teacher is the best judge, but we trust that the examples that follow will prove a useful "tool kit" to all teachers. The words in BOLD SMALL CAPITALS throughout will be explained in greater detail in Act Three: Managing a Drama (pages 51). They are useful Drama techniques that any teacher can apply in the classroom.

## GETTING STARTED

COMMON CONCERN:

### So what's Drama about, then?

SUGGESTION:

### Conflict.

Essentially, Drama is about people with problems. When we use the word "drama," this notion is always implicit. Drama is about people in conflict, but this can range from the most momentous of physical contests

15

CHILDREN CAN REPRESENT OBJECTS AS WELL AS PEOPLE: HERE THEY FORM
THE FETTERS AND BONDS THAT RESTRAIN A PRISONER.

to internal struggles of individuals and groups. Consider the following dramatic situation:

> There must have been twenty thousand charging toward their ranks.
> The thin line of soldiers looked uneasily at each other as the enemy
> rushed ever closer. . . .

And, at the other end of the dramatic spectrum:

> Little Red Riding Hood saw the flowers. They looked pretty. Her
> grandmother would love them. It wouldn't do any harm to leave the
> path for just a few short steps, would it? But, then again, her mother
> had said not to. . . .

The conflicts, whether great or small, can be either internal or external,
or both.

COMMON CONCERN:

**How do I get started?**

SUGGESTION:

**Formulate a question as your starting point and stimulus.**

The question is a way of introducing your students to the idea of Drama (see also TWILIGHTING, page 83). The question will always be a "what if" of some kind or other. It might be an indirect question, such as:

> "If you were a group of explorers in 1995 (or indeed, Romans in 56 B.C., or Vikings in 794 A.D.) undertaking an expedition, what sort of preparations do you think you might have to make?"

or

> "If you were Daedalus, the Greek inventor, working out how to construct a flying machine, what might your first ideas look like?"

The purpose of the question is to create an exciting focus and an impetus for finding out more, i.e., an incentive to create a learning "narrative" or "text." The question sets up the problem; for Drama, by definition, is always problematic. Possibly, when the time is right, a more direct kind of question can be adopted.

Example:

> "We are about to order a meal in a French restaurant. What do you need to think about saying before calling the waiter?"

or

> "Our kid was offered some drugs at the disco last night. I'm worried about it. What do you think I should do?"

COMMON CONCERN:

**Now what?**

SUGGESTION:

**Set the scene together.**

A positive strength of Drama is that we can play with time, going forward or back or even stopping it to consider an event in detail.

There is nothing to prevent a teacher from saying, at any stage in the lesson, "I think we need to know a little more about where our action is taking place."

To draw an analogy with a theatre play, there is a set, however minimal, against which a drama is enacted. In this context we, the audience, all see the same set. Similarly in a Drama lesson, we may sometimes need to establish where our play is taking place. But because we do not "see" it in quite the same way as in a theatre, we set up an imaginary meeting of minds.

At this stage, resources and research can be applied to provide further background information and deepen involvement. It would be useful, for example, when talking about a medieval castle or a scientific laboratory, to have material available to assist in this "scene-setting" process, e.g., maps, plans, pictures, diagrams, measurements, etc. There may, of course, be instances where the scene can be taken for granted, such as if the drama is taking place in a school very like our own. "Scene-setting" can quite legitimately take place before the opening question is asked; for teachers may well feel that they want students to know more about the subject matter before embarking on the actual Drama itself. While this approach is perfectly valid, it is worth mentioning that the advantage of posing the question at the outset is that exciting questions can frequently provide a stimulus to finding things out.

SUGGESTION:

**Decide who's who.**

The process is similar with people: as a playwright, for example, fleshes out characters, so teachers and students may need to think about the people in their Drama "text" before proceeding any further. This strategy is painstaking, but it is part of a determining process from which quality will come. It is worth noting that it:

- enables teachers to assess students' experiences and understanding of the subject of the Drama, to determine their learning needs, and to plan teaching responses to pupil reactions;
- builds commitment and engagement in what the class and teacher are doing;
- encourages the exploration of what motivates people within the drama (and in real life as well; see ROLE ON THE WALL, page 80);
- lays a foundation for dramatic narrative.

COMMON CONCERN:

**Hang on a minute! My children aren't used to this. Their behavior may suffer.**

SUGGESTION:

**Establish ground rules.**

Children need to agree with you to a basic code of conduct in Drama. They should agree that:

- they take their work seriously;
- they respect one another;
- they trust one another;
- everyone is entitled to a hearing;
- on an agreed signal or instruction from the teacher (e.g., "Freeze!" or "Cut!") the activity immediately stops and all are silent.

COMMON CONCERN:

**But mightn't it all be rather strange and alarming?**

SUGGESTION:

**Build on resources already in use in the classroom, such as photos and pictures.**

Use photos or pictures as stimuli and starting points for your questions. Of the picture below, for example, you might ask:

"Who are the people in this picture? Where are they?"
"What are they doing? What are they thinking?"
"What will happen next?"
"What were they doing five minutes ago?"
"Do they know each other? How can you tell?"
"When was this picture taken? How can you tell?"
"What sort of background do they come from?"

In this way, we establish and consolidate interest in the stimulus material and lay the foundations for dramatic development.

A picture can be set up three dimensionally using students in a **STILL IMAGE;** then techniques like **IMPROVISATION, THOUGHT TRACKING,** and **NARRA-**

DOG, SIR? WHAT DOG?

TIVE (see pages 75, 78, 75, and 81) can be applied to develop the activity further.

SUGGESTION:

**Focus on particularly dramatic moments in a story, novel, or play.**

Create images (see STILL IMAGE, page 75) and play out with students what they think might happen next. Their text can then be compared with the author's and they can speculate on and hypothesize about the reasons for the similarities or differences.

COMMON CONCERN:

**If I pick a moment in the middle of a story that the children already know, isn't there a danger they'll just "act out" the story as it is?**

SUGGESTION:

**Make your instructions and questions clear.**

To avoid possible confusion, say openly something like: "I know that after this point Humpty Dumpty was attended by the king's men, but what else might happen, do you think?"

Confusion arises only if the students think they have to guess the response they think their teacher wants, or that it is necessary to stick to the existing narrative.

SUGGESTION:

**You might also try using classroom displays . . .**

Classroom displays lend themselves to dramatic starting points, just as photos do. A model train set could be the starting point for a Drama about the people traveling on the train, or waiting on the platform for it. We might formulate a question like, "What are the thoughts of the different passengers as a delay is announced?"

Alternatively, we might set up a STILL IMAGE of what the waiting people think might have happened to the train.

SUGGESTION:

**. . . or PRETEND CORNERS . . .**

There is a plethora of play and dramatic activity already taking place in the PRETEND CORNER. The crucial issues are concerned with how this area is set up and when the teacher should intervene. (See page 97 on PRETEND CORNERS.)

SUGGESTION:

**. . . or toys . . .**

Focus on a favorite toy to start a drama:

> "Why do you think teddy is so sad? How can we make him/her happy?"

For older students:

> "This is the gun that was found at the scene of the crime. What forensics tests should we carry out to help our investigations?"

SUGGESTION:

**. . . or video.**

As with a story, we can use a video to focus on dramatic moments, analyze what is going on and explore what might happen. The dramatic focus enables students to explore issues, implications, and ideas in a creative mode.

COMMON CONCERN:

**What part do I play in these starting points?**

SUGGESTION:

**TEACHER IN ROLE.**

This technique is only an extension of the opening example cited in answer to "How do I get started?" except that within TEACHER IN ROLE (see page

74), the teacher plays a part as well. In formulating an opening question, there are three simple considerations:

1. Who are the students going to be?
2. Who is the teacher going to be?
3. What is the problem?

Example:

"Fellow Athenians, the Persian army of one million soldiers is but a hundred miles from the city. As clerk to the assembly, I beg you to tell me what orders I am to convey to the military."

Such a question establishes the role the teacher is to play, as well as those of the students. It is important to note that this opening question is also an open one (see "Asking Questions," page 60).

COMMON CONCERN:

**Not roleplay! I'm not being a tree for anyone!**

SUGGESTION:

**Don't panic.**

We all have had bad experiences of the "being a tree" variety and having, mercifully, torn up those roots most of us, quite reasonably, have no desire to be repotted. So what does TEACHER IN ROLE mean and entail? The role played is entirely in the teacher's hands. It can be low-key, using a doll or toy as above.

Example:

"I've heard that you're very helpful people. My baby is crying. Do you know what I should do?"

Here teacher is essentially him or herself in an imaginary situation. More daringly, perhaps, teacher might ask: "What would you like me to do in the Health Center/Aztec pyramid/Native American village/power station we are setting up? Fine, I will be a receptionist/priest/elder/technician, but you will have to tell me what needs to be done as I am quite old, but not very senior." (See MANTLE OF THE EXPERT, page 74.)

In each instance, the teacher's role is informed by the students' responses. It is quite a good idea to choose a low-status role so that students do not feel the need to defer to the teacher in role all the time. Within this strategy, students are encouraged to take responsibility more easily. Even though the second example cites potentially high-status roles, each requires help and advice. (See also page 28.)

COMMON CONCERN:

**But how will my students know whether I'm "in role" or not?**

SUGGESTION:

**Tell them.**

Younger children rarely have difficulty with the concept of role. They change roles constantly in their play and they have learned to recognize signals indicating role and to act on them very quickly. Adults, however, tend to be far more concerned about this issue than children are. At the outset it might be advisable to establish grounds rules about teacher's role.

Example:

"When I sit in this chair, I am the Chancellor of the Exchequer (or the Queen; or Adrian Mole, aged thirteen and three-quarters), and when I stand up, I'm your teacher."

COMMON CONCERN:

**I have difficulty going into and coming out of role as well. What can I do to address this problem?**

SUGGESTION:

**Use a more objective strategy.**

All right, rather than say, "Let's be Irish immigrants (or Leonardo da Vinci and his students)," try another tack.

Example:

"As historians (or scientists) we need to find out about emigration from Ireland (or the principles of flight). Let us investigate the data that is available and see what conclusions can be drawn."

or

"We are making a film about the remarkable antislavery activist, Harriet Tubman. Let us research her life from her childhood to her role as secret agent and daring commando leader and then we will put together scenes from her life."

This latter example has the advantage of considering the potential and application of the cinematic art form and also opens up other potential avenues in media education as well as historical and dramatic issues. It might also prove a more appropriate and constructive approach to take with older students (see FRAMING, page 80).

COMMON CONCERN:

**How dramatic do I have to be?**

SUGGESTION:

**Decide as you see fit.**

Some teachers actually enjoy taking on more overtly dramatic roles for themselves and may wish to signal their role by changing their voice with an accent or an appropriate style of speaking. Children can be responsive to this strategy, but attention needs to be paid to the danger of the teacher dominating the drama in this way. It is perfectly feasible within this format and frequently useful for teachers to use their "normal" voices to reflect and comment on what is happening within the drama.

It is also the case that, having agreed upon a role with the students—e.g., "Shall I be a giant in the play?"—the statement alone is often sufficient and that there is no need to maintain a "giant" voice. (Teachers probably are "giants" in reality to small children.)

COMMON CONCERN:

**What other strategies or techniques can be used?**

SUGGESTION:

**Use props.**

Simple props, like a crown, a walking stick, a chair (as a throne), a cloak, can be extremely effective in delineating role for teachers and students. After all, we are dealing with an artistic medium where symbol and ritual assume heightened meaning and power. It is also worth remembering that within

this medium it is often useful not to reveal one's symbol or prop immediately but to play with the magic of possibility.

Example:

"Inside this box is the most important object in the kingdom. I wonder if I dare show it to you?"

or

"I have a very important letter in this envelope. Can anyone suggest what it might be about and who might have sent it?"

Questions of this nature can engage and stimulate positive responses.

COMMON CONCERN:

**You are talking about my joining in. Won't this mean that I lose control?**

SUGGESTION:

**Not if you are clear on your role and its purpose.**

The use of role often enables the teacher to maintain control over the proceedings. It is possible, through roleplay, to strengthen dramatic impact and to reinforce concentration and commitment simultaneously, e.g., "I cannot believe that at a time like this, when our village (or the emperor, or our research establishment or our community center) is threatened by Cortez and his army (or by Britons/by government cuts/by developers), some of our people (legionnaires/scientists/friends/neighbors) are giggling at the edge of our meeting (in the ranks/at their work tables/in the seats at the back).

COMMON CONCERN:

**What about my status?**

SUGGESTION:

**Be positive about the ways in which Drama can enhance your status.**

While a teacher's status in the drama may be "low" to encourage and elicit a more forthcoming response from students, this does not mean prejudicing one's control over the proceedings. Because the teacher is operating within a carefully structured, negotiated process, the status and role of teacher and pupil should always be clearly delineated.

Students also tend to be most responsive to their teacher when s/he participates in their learning.

## DEVELOPMENT

COMMON CONCERN:

**You haven't mentioned drama games and warm-ups. Doesn't drama always begin with them?**

SUGGESTION:

**Not necessarily. Try to use games and exercises in a context, and only where they are needed or useful.**

Games and exercises are very useful means of breaking the ice, stimulating dramatic activity, and helping interaction to take place.

A warm-up itself, however, has little value unless the participants understand why they are doing it. It is important for the teacher to explain why a particular game needs to be played.

Example:

"We are not working well together at the moment, so let's play a game that will improve our ability to cooperate."

or

"We cannot do this drama unless we know each other's names, so let's play a name game for a few minutes to help us."

Games and exercises should therefore be used at appropriate moments to enhance and inform the drama in a way that is contextualized and relevant to the learning. Otherwise, they may simply be a distraction. (See **GAMES AND EXERCISES,** pages 84.)

Of course, regular cooperative game sessions can be of enormous value to the social and personal development of a class, quite apart from the context of teaching Drama.

COMMON CONCERN:

**I can see my students being interested in this way of working, but I foresee problems.**

SUGGESTION:

**Be specific. Let's identify some concerns.**

COMMON CONCERN:

**I have tried similar ideas in the school hall, but the students got overexcited. What can I do about it?**

SUGGESTION:

**Limit the space you work in until you and your students are ready for more.**

In "Drama in School: The Stage You're At" (page 7), we said that it was feasible at the most developed end of the continuum for drama to be used in the classroom like reading and writing. If this ideal is to be realized, then Drama should be seen as an activity that fits into the classroom space and does not always require the use of a gymnasium or hall.

Some space is necessary, but in most instances desks can be put to the side of the room to create a working area. If space is still limited or inadequate, think about focusing on confined situations, such as elevators, caves, prisons, dungeons, holds of ships, offices, space shuttles, as possible contexts for Drama, and make speech and sound (cf. radio Drama) the format for the work.

When space is at a premium, rather than set up **STILL IMAGES** in the room, students can "storyboard" moments from a dramatic narrative. Using a strip cartoon format also has the potential advantage of being a permanent record to be displayed or used for assessment purposes.

If the hall is used, try working in a smaller part of it by cordoning a space off with chairs or benches. This makes it easier to manage a group and structure a lesson within a larger area. As the children get used to the activity, the space can be expanded, as appropriate. The teacher always has to feel comfortable with the setup, so increase or decrease the physical space whenever you feel the need.

COMMON CONCERN:

**What if the hall or gym is normally used as a thoroughfare for other lessons?**

SUGGESTION:

**Communicate your intentions to all staff.**

Ensure that the whole staff (teaching and nonteaching) know that the hall or gym is going to be used for Drama. Negotiate timings with staff beforehand. Insist that the children's work be taken seriously and valued—e.g., people cannot walk through a Drama lesson any more than they would stroll through a room where any other lesson was taking place. Ensure that Drama is put on the timetable for the use of the space.

COMMON CONCERN:

**How should students dress?**

SUGGESTION:

**It's up to you.**

Drama is a basic way of working, and therefore ought to take place with a minimum of fuss. There may, however, be occasions when the dramatic activity might involve stretching or bending. In these instances students should dress for comfort and not feel restricted by their clothing. Teachers should make their own judgments about what suits their students' needs.

COMMON CONCERN:

**Should students sit on the floor, or on benches or chairs?**

SUGGESTION:

**What is most appropriate for your class and this drama?**

The physicality of the learning space is of crucial importance. Comfort is obviously a concern, but teachers should also be aware that students need to see each other, hear each other, engage with each other, and be involved in and interact with the drama that is taking place. Seating students in a circle fulfills these requirements and provides a dynamic performance space in the middle of which everyone can focus and to which all can react.

COMMON CONCERN:

**I take the point about the circle, but give me a sense of how it might work in practice?**

SUGGESTION:

**Keep it simple.**

At the start, it is useful to structure activities that are easily manageable within the circle and are teacher-led. For example, the teacher, in role as steward of a Norman baron, might say:

> "Before we plan our invasion of England, let us consider the jobs and responsibilities each of us has in our own village, and out of that, decide what function each person will fulfill on the expedition."

As the students respond, s/he writes their responses down on a sheet of paper as a focus for planning. Similarly, the topography and an artistic representation of what constitutes the village might be drawn within the circle, initially by the teacher.

COMMON CONCERN:

**What about children who don't say anything, or are self-conscious?**

SUGGESTION:

**Vary the dynamic.**

Ask the students to discuss their ideas together in twos and threes and come up with an agreed response. Drama is a social medium. Stress that we need to come up with ways of working that give everyone a voice, not just the confident. Don't push too hard at first, but give students the opportunity to see that they will not be put on the spot or exposed if they do not respond immediately. Manipulate groupings if necessary, but basically relax. They will join in eventually if they see that the atmosphere is right.

COMMON CONCERN:

**What if students have to touch each other as part of the drama? My children couldn't cope with that.**

SUGGESTION:

**Let the drama take the strain.** (See GAMES AND EXERCISES, page 84.)

Unless a child has a deeper psychological reason for not wanting to touch or be touched, inhibitions about being physically at ease with one another are perhaps best countered by the demands of the drama without forcing anything. In other words, if one character has to touch another to cross a perilous rope bridge, for example, then it's their story—can they make it work?

An alternative strategy is to play some high-energy physical games such as cooperative musical hoops (a variation of musical chairs). As in the traditional game, all players move around the playing space to some form of music, avoiding a number of hoops (safer than chairs) scattered across the floor. The music is suddenly stopped and all the players step inside one of the hoops, perhaps two or three in each hoop initially. The controller of the game then removes one of the hoops, starts the music again, and repeats the process. As the game goes on, more and more people have to crowd into fewer and fewer hoops. Unlike traditional musical chairs, the object of this version is to keep everyone *in* the game even when all but one or two hoops have been removed. Then when the music stops for the last time the whole class is huddled tightly together trying to balance in the remaining hoop or hoops, helping each other to stay within them. It is difficult to be stand-offish under those circumstances.

COMMON CONCERN:

**What if students make fun of each other?**

SUGGESTION:

**Remind them of the ground rules.**

A good laugh makes for happy learning, and Drama should not be perceived as a solemn activity. However, we must as teachers insist that students take their work seriously. Nobody can be expected to engage in a drama if they are concerned that they may be mocked or that what they say may be ridiculed. Trust is an essential ground rule that may have to be agreed upon at the outset or negotiated when the occasion arises. Games may also prove useful in engendering trust.

It is also essential that students recognize that Drama deals with fictions. Therefore, when we create drama with our students, we must insist that fictional names and characters are invented for the people who are taking center stage at the time. The actors should not be exposed to derision, nor should people outside the immediacy of the group, whether they are students, teachers, caretakers, etc. If people cannot be safe within a role, then we cannot expect the shy to participate, nor the extrovert to explore fully and freely the issues under consideration.

COMMON CONCERN:

**What about the child nobody wants to work with?**

SUGGESTION:

**Refer to the ground rules.**

Drama cannot work if there isn't cooperation with and between students. Stress that leaving people out is not an option you can countenance. Use helpful, caring, respected, and cooperative students to support your actions. Use the drama to consolidate this approach.

We talked before about how the assumption of high-status roles by teachers might lead to their dominating the drama (see also TEACHER IN ROLE, page 74). Try putting the isolated student in a high-status role to which the rest of the group must defer, in order to give such students a dominant voice and to help enhance their status outside the drama as well.

In instances of this sort, teachers must monitor what happens, skillfully and sensitively. Apply a variety of methods in bringing this strategy to bear. Another possibility might be to assign the rest of the group roles as scribes or advisers/supporters of the child in question. Intervene where you feel it is necessary in selecting groups to work together.

COMMON CONCERN:

**What about the noise?**

SUGGESTION:

**Well, there is noise, and then there's *NOISE!***

Just because Educational Drama is active and expressive, it doesn't have to be noisy. While it is true that the children may be acting something out that creates some noise, it must be remembered that this has to occur within a

structured framework. There are strategies that can be applied that under-line the control of the situation. If, for example, the action being dramatized is likely to be noisy, suggest that it be carried out in slow motion or mimed. Sometimes noise will occur, but make a distinction between creative noise and foolery. Where the school is open-plan, it is advisable to discuss what you intend to do with colleagues beforehand if you feel that the children may be more vociferous than usual.

There is no reason, however, that Drama should be noisier than any other subject or way of working.

COMMON CONCERN:

**What if they cannot get used to this way of working?**

SUGGESTION:

**Work around the altercations.**

It is true that Drama deals with physical and mental conflict and sometimes it will be felt necessary for this to be expressed in violent activity. This is a major concern for teachers, principally because it can develop into an uncon-trolled, dangerous, free-for-all. We want to avoid this at all costs. Accord-ingly, try using the following techniques to deal with fights, wars, revolutions, executions, and any other situations where loss of life and/or limb is on the cards.

- Look at the moments before or after "fights" occur. This is usually where the real drama is, anyway. Work on and emphasize eye contact, the implications of violence, and the feelings of the combatants. Essentially, slow down the action and get students to think the process through.
- Recreate a fight, its antecedents or aftermath, by using STILL IMAGES (see page 75). These can be the focus for group discussions and interaction.
- Look at stage combat techniques. Stress that discipline and control is necessary for safe and effective presentations.
- Narrate the fight and ask the participants to go through the motions of the fighting in slow motion as you describe what is happening. Stylize the activity.

At all times, stress the importance of form and the absolute need for control.

COMMON CONCERN:

**What if students are still naughty?**

**Refer to school procedure.**

Drama is no different from other subjects. Normal discipline procedures still apply in Drama lessons. Drama's significant contribution lies in the fact that it is a form that positively encourages active, interacting, negotiated, imaginative, reflective, and creative learning, all of which calls for a high degree of discipline and self-control.

COMMON CONCERN:

**What about "overinvolvement" of a gentler nature, e.g., the death of a pet in the Drama?**

SUGGESTION:

**Stop the action.**

You can, of course, stop the drama at any time if you feel it is necessary (see comments on ground rules, page 19). Emphasize that we are only pretending, but use students' reactions positively where it is possible in order to explore how people feel in real situations and how they can come to terms with and cope with them.

COMMON CONCERN:

**What if I want to create a still image or short plays in separate groups? How will they cope with that? How will I manage it?**

SUGGESTION.

**Explain and demonstrate the process and try it out beforehand.**

In the middle of the circle, set up the STILL IMAGE in a gradual and structured way, using one person at a time and asking others to join in until the image is created for all to see. Involve those who are on the outside in the developing process. Those who watch should be seen as an active and not a passive audience. Ask the watchers to provide suggestions, comments (positive), and analysis of what the STILL IMAGE signifies; get them to "read" what is happening and interpret subtle changes in positions. They might invent the thoughts of particular characters in the STILL IMAGE (see THOUGHT TRACKING, page 75) or advise and support characters in coming up with lines to say, attitudes to assume, or body language to adopt (see TIME OUT, page 80). When the students see the learning dynamic is supportive, cooperative, and structured, and they appreciate and understand how they have to work, try letting them explore ideas in separate groups.

## What if they cannot get used to this way of working?

SUGGESTION:

## Persevere.

It may take a while for the process to be assimilated. Teachers should emphasize the need for all to work together. If problems occur while groups work separately, use the plenary format of the circle to voice concerns, give feedback, and come up with agreed solutions and resolutions. At this stage the teacher may have to intervene and explain more often to ensure that the working method is made absolutely clear. Do not push too hard too soon.

COMMON CONCERN:

## My little ones get bored easily.

SUGGESTION:

## Vary the activity.

The key is to take it gently and not force the pace if the students are not ready. Learners of all ages need a variety of experience if they are not to become restless. Pep up energy levels by involving everyone if something interesting is offered by a pupil. For example, if someone does an effective digging mime, why not have everyone get on their feet and have them do the

same thing? This can, if necessary, be controlled by slow motion. It can be augmented by the addition of a sound effect (made by the children) as they dig. A song might be introduced to accompany their activity. The teacher has three options at this stage.

1. to develop this activity more fully, such as into a dance/drama
2. to return to the original narrative
3. to make a note of it and develop it at a later stage

Because we are dealing with an art form and the creation of resonant images, and because Drama is about doing and setting things up and not merely discussing them, there is every chance that an activity like the above will be easily and vividly called to mind if the teacher chooses to refer to it later.

COMMON CONCERN:

**If and when they go into groups and work on their own, should they return to the circle and perform for everyone else?**

SUGGESTION:

**Yes, but . . .**

Children like showing their work to their peers and their teacher, but there are problems in seeing many groups' work at one time. An important element of any learning is reflection and there is a danger that this will be absent if we merely watch group after group without discussing, analyzing and refining their work. It can also be boring. Children's work in this context tends to be stereotypical, and it may be appropriate for the teacher and students to challenge (in a positive way) what they see. Merely running through ideas, then, without reflection and critical analysis can reinforce bad practice and unsound, ill-considered ideas. In setting up a circle as the working format, we are suggesting a dynamic that invites active contributions from the audience on what is presented to them.

Teachers should also bear in mind that scenes that have been improvised are often difficult to recreate and actors within such scenes can be more pre-occupied with what to say next rather than with the meaning, form, and context of the piece as a whole (see IMPROVISATION, page 78). A plenary session offers a forum for each group to report back on its problems with the contents or with the way of working. The teacher might choose to impose a time limit on the scene to be represented or possibly suggest a STILL IMAGE of what the group considers to be its most significant moment.

Alternatively the scene could be expanded to, say, three STILL IMAGES. If appropriate, these images can be "brought to life" (see VIDEO TRACKING, page 78). Starting or ending a scene with a STILL IMAGE can be a useful control mechanism in improvisation or small group play making.

Where there is dialogue, it might help if each player in a scene is restricted to one sentence, one phrase, or even one word.

COMMON CONCERN:

**Should this take place on a stage, if there is one?**

SUGGESTION:

**Think about this carefully.**

Students often like performing on a stage. They can be seen. They look just like real actors. A Drama lesson, however, is not just about theatre product, with a play, a cast, and an audience. It is about learning. Performance is a vital part of the learning process as we use this element to concentrate our minds on situations, explore them, reflect on them, and learn from them. It is perhaps more useful, however, to view a lesson that uses Drama as a kind of play rehearsal where we try out ideas, work on them together, investigate motivation, invent, practice, refine, and hone our dialogues without risk or threat. Later, the "texts" we have created can be applied to the experiences of the real work. As the rehearsal/lesson progresses, we perform in order to represent and test our ideas. With this sort of emphasis, performance is clearly not our prime objective. If the stage is to be used, teachers should bear in mind the above considerations.

COMMON CONCERN:

## What about school plays and assemblies? Should they be scripted or devised?

SUGGESTION:

## The choice is yours. Try and see what works better for you.

School plays and Drama within assemblies make a vital contribution to the life of the school. Clearly, they can emerge from a variety of different approaches, and teachers and pupils have to make their own decisions about what suits them. There are two significant questions that we should pose with regard to school plays and assembly performances:

1. How are they related to the curriculum?
2. Have they kept up with good educational practice in other areas of the curriculum?

It could well be argued that if plays (and assemblies) spring out of and are integrated with the curriculum as a whole they have clearly identifiable and valuable curricular aims. In such instances, Drama supports and resources other subjects as they support and resource Drama. An assembly on bullying or healthy eating, for example, has direct relevance to both the curriculum and the whole school ethos. This has obvious implications for Drama's place in the school, and for its untapped inservice potential, particularly with reference to problem solving, teamwork, and management. Whatever the subject matter, it is important that the staff, students, and parents (see "Drama and Parent-School Partnerships," page 129) do not see plays and assemblies as disconnected, on-off treats that have no specific relevance to their experiences in and out of school.

Plays and assemblies can be devised out of the content of lessons using the strategies outlined elsewhere. Teachers and students may select, redraft, and develop moments from their investigations of particular issues and themes. These can serve as foundations on which to base and build future play and assembly texts.

The mounting of any school production can also be the focus for a range of cross-curricular work that resources the "stage" activity—i.e., lighting; set design, construction, and painting; costume and props (design and manufacture); writing of scripts and sound (music and effects).

In addition, it serves to underscore learning through "front of house" activities like marketing, publicity (Media and Business Studies), tickets, posters, and programs (artwork, layout, and desktop publishing), box office (Math and Information Technology), and catering (intermission food and drinks).

A SCENE PAINTER PREPARES.

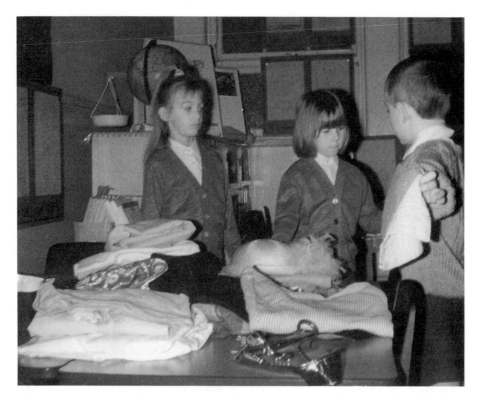

A COSTUME DEPARTMENT AT WORK.

COMMON CONCERN:

**How do you prevent this kind of work being overdirected by the teacher?**

SUGGESTION:

**There is always room for open questions.**

The lesson-management structure suggested in the course of this "tool kit" is initially focused by the teacher. This is because the way of working has to be enunciated with clarity and control by teachers, but there should always be room for negotiation and dialogue between teachers and students. The teacher's responsibility is to check at all stages that the students understand the implications of the suggestions or choices they have made. For example, having decided to locate a scene within, say, an African village, the planning might well take place on a large sheet of paper, and the teacher might well ask, "You've said you wanted a river in this village. Well, what will happen to this road (indicating a road that has already been decided on) that comes up against it?"

"Build a bridge!" might well be the response.

The teacher might then choose to question this choice and persuade students to think it through.

"What is the bridge to be made of?"

"Wood," comes the reply.

"Where is the wood to come from, as we have no forest on our map?"

The location of the forest is then chosen and a whole set of new jobs set in train to service the building of the bridge. We have also opened up the possibility of considering other implications, such as logistics, resource management, and the environmental side-effects of the construction. Through the process of open questioning, the teacher and students deepen their commitment to and understanding of the background for the drama they are creating.

This simple expedient, however, has unearthed the potential for making informed choices about a whole range of subjects and has exposed the hidden costs of decision making (see "Asking Questions," page 60).

COMMON CONCERN:

**How much of the drama should I plan?**

SUGGESTION:

**The beginning should be carefully worked out and possible developments identified.**

The initial question must be carefully devised and matched to pupil experience. What happens after that should be anticipated and not predicted (see "Principles and Process," page 53). The teacher should have a sense of direction and not a fixed agenda.

Inevitably there will be specific areas of learning and matters of content that have to be covered, but the children should come to it through their teacher's application of structure and an awareness of the students' needs and not a rigorous adhesion to their plans.

COMMON CONCERN:

## Whose agenda is it, then?

SUGGESTION:

## It is a mutual agenda.

If students are to develop through any educational activity, they must have some stake in the agenda. Dramatic performance is sometimes seen as a director's medium. Educational Drama is concerned with students' learning, knowledge, and understanding, and as such, the agenda of the drama has to be negotiated with the key people in the equation—the learners.

COMMON CONCERN:

## How can I make use of drama to assess my students?

SUGGESTION:

## Consider Drama's process.

Drama encourages teachers to assess their children and children to assess each other. Within a Drama lesson students should be encouraged to work independently of their teacher. When students are working together the teacher can circulate, intervene, challenge, and facilitate. Drama enables teachers to monitor and assess students' work in a positive, exciting framework and ideally places them to learn about students' attainment and needs. It should be noted that in order to structure a Drama lesson effectively, teachers need to address several key questions:

What have they shown me that they know, think, and feel?
What have they learned?
What do they want to learn?
What do I judge that they need to learn?

These questions are essential elements of the assessment process as well.

COMMON CONCERN:

## What about evidence of development in Drama?

SUGGESTION:

## Don't worry too much about levels and targets.

Students who use Drama regularly will, in due course, demonstrate an ability to work cooperatively, creatively, and confidently. Speaking and listening skills will also be enhanced. Many people feel it is inappropriate, however, to predict (for example) that students of particular ages will be able to perform specific tasks at specific levels. Within a Drama, five- and six-year-olds are often able to negotiate, work artistically, and exhibit a range and awareness of dramatic conventions such as ritual and symbol beyond their teacher's expectations. These developments can be recorded in a variety of ways, e.g., audio and video tapes and anthologies of written and drawn material.

COMMON CONCERN:

## Say we recreate a journey for younger students or explore an encounter in a community center with older ones—isn't this just experiential play, and not dramatic?

SUGGESTION:

## Teacher intervention recreates dramatic elements.

A Drama lesson is, in essence, concerned with the creation of a play "text" in a similar way to a theatre piece. A play that is one-paced would be unlikely to engage its audience, and so the playwright constructs changes of rhythm and introduces moments of tension. Our key opening question serves to outline the nature of the problem to be considered, and this has the function of creating an immediate point of interest for the students. This tension is what propels the drama from the outset, and it is, by definition, part of Drama's very nature. At various stages, however, the pace and engagement may flag. It may well need a fresh injection of tension to rebuild a sense of place, problem, and time, and teachers may feel they have to intervene to refocus and reactivate the participants in the drama. This intervention may be handled in a fairly objective, but nonetheless dramatic, way.

Example:

Three (fictional) weeks had passed since the Vikings started to prepare for their expedition, but that night Thor's Priestess called them all together and told them that they had to catch the evening tide before the storm came down off the mountain. In the stillness of the evening, as the flickering fires reflected on the faces of the villagers, they all thought of the journey that they were soon to undertake. . . .

Alternatively, the teacher might announce that s/he was going into role, and they must all listen carefully. . . .

> "Put down your chainsaws for a moment and come and listen. The foreman lumberjack was clearing a new path over there, and this poisoned dart missed his head by inches. We were assured there wouldn't be any risks on this job!"

In each instance, the teacher signals that a new urgency is to be imposed on the drama and the responsibility for taking it on rests with the student roleplayers. This intervention also offers the possibility of moving into several cross-curricular areas—such as Math:

> "Shipmates, I have the coordinates from Columbus' log here. Let us work out exactly where we are. As far as I'm concerned, something certainly doesn't add up!"

COMMON CONCERN:

**Can this methodology work with Special Needs students?**

SUGGESTION:

**Very much so.**

SEVENTY PUPILS AND TWENTY TEACHERS STAGE A SPECIAL NEEDS/ MAINSTREAM PROJECT ON NATIVE AMERICANS.

A WHEELCHAIR IS INTEGRATED INTO A PRODUCTION ON DINOSAURS.

Special Needs students are especially responsive to this way of working. The principles and practice of working with Special Needs students are the same as in any other Educational Drama context. Teachers need to be especially conscious, however, of appropriateness of language and stimulus material.

At the outset, it is particularly vital that the teacher closely monitor the Special Needs students' perceptions and understanding. For example, teachers in mainstream may, perhaps, more readily assume that their students understand that zoo animals, as represented by toys or pictures in books, are not really that size because they appreciate the essential principles of scale. This may not be the case with some Special Needs students, and so teacher awareness is particularly relevant. TEACHER IN ROLE, however, is one method of assisting and underscoring a sympathetic and sensitive approach.

A class of children with poor motor skills can improve and practice these in a nonthreatening context when teacher explains s/he is in role as:

> A circus performer who has forgotten how to walk the tightrope (bench)
> and in consequence has been thrown out of the circus. Can they help
> him (her) learn those skills again?

Children find it easier to practice and demonstrate the skills of movement in this context because dramatic narrative has relieved the pressure on them and focused on "the performer's" problem. In being distanced from their particular concerns through roleplay they are helped to address, work, and improve on them in safety and security.

COMMON CONCERN:

## How should I use drama with advanced students?

SUGGESTION:

## To underscore your present way of working.

Drama is a very useful medium for exploring literature texts, characters, motivation, and issues. It is crucial to consolidate academic approaches to texts by active methods (see the discussion of texts in Act Five), such as creating and presenting scenes from plays, poems, and novels, and focusing on their form, meaning, and interpretation. While this has obvious relevance for English, dramatic approaches provide fertile strategies in, for example, History, Art, and Science teaching as well. Approaching a History, Art, or Science project in role and in the context of a challenging fiction can stimulate students to see things afresh, in new and unexpected ways. Moreover, the inevitable collaboration that Drama entails leads to questions and insights that individual students might never arrive at alone. Drama, at any level, allows us to work out in a positive, immediate, and stimulating way why events happen and what alternatives to action (or inaction) are feasible and advisable. As stated above, variety of presentation can enliven and activate learning, and ultimately is a profitable investment in time.

COMMON CONCERN:

## How long should a drama activity last?

SUGGESTION:

## From five minutes to infinity.

When one is just starting to employ Drama, it is a good idea to experiment for just a short time, such as by introducing some Drama into a story (see above).

As teachers become more confident and feel it is manageable, and that students have a grasp of the ground rules and the working method, they may choose to expand the time spent incrementally. Some teachers use Drama all the time across the curriculum, five days a week!

Make your own judgments!

COMMON CONCERN:

## What if it all falls apart?

SUGGESTION:

## Be open.

If things don't work, don't plow on, regardless. Negotiations in Drama are two way. Is there any way in which your students can help you? Where did it go wrong?

Review and reflect on the experience. Was everything clear? Were the ground rules adequately laid out?

When trying out new ideas, keep to a manageable period of time and have a fall-back idea in case students are unresponsive. Move into another medium, such as drawing or writing. They can still write diaries, journals, and poems "in role," and so it might be retrievable on further analysis. Refer again to this "Teacher's Tool Kit."

# Act Three

# MANAGING A DRAMA

## — PART ONE —
## PRINCIPLES

### THE CONFIDENCE TO TAKE RISKS

To take part in a drama is to be willing to take risks. "What might we do if . . ." is like stepping out onto an exposed rock face. It involves risking new ideas, testing values and attitudes, trying out different emotional responses, rehearsing unfamiliar dialogues *in public.* Climbers will take risks, but only if they know those risks are within a proper margin of safety. That confidence comes from being well prepared and aware of the terrain. What follows is an outline of one set of preparations and awarenesses for Drama in education.

### *1. Learners' Own Experiences*

The process has to start with the learners at the center (see Figure 1, "The Ring of Confidence"). It has to, because we know that children make sense of new ideas only by attempting to integrate them into the scheme of ideas they already possess. The first step in the Drama process is, then, for the teacher to acknowledge, as far as is possible, what the learners already know. This means accepting, whether we approve of them or not, their perceptions, their values, their understandings—their experiences.

Sometimes they will demonstrate that they have insufficient experience to even start a particular drama. A child with severe learning difficulties, down on his knees sweeping something imaginary and very small into a cap laid on the floor after a drama about farming, explains he is "putting the

IN A "MINING DISASTER," CHILDREN RESCUE THEIR TEACHER IN ROLE.

**Principles and Process**

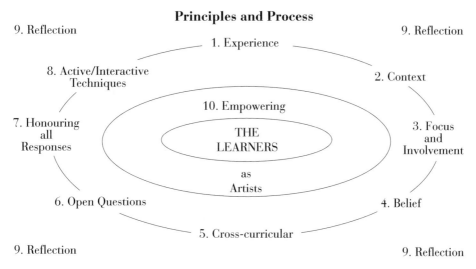

9. Reflection                                                  9. Reflection

1. Experience

8. Active/Interactive
Techniques                                            2. Context

10. Empowering

7. Honouring
all           THE           3. Focus
Responses    LEARNERS     and
                                 Involvement

as
Artists

6. Open Questions                               4. Belief

5. Cross-curricular

9. Reflection                                                    9. Reflection

FIGURE 1. THE RING OF CONFIDENCE

pigs away now." The following week we all visit the City Farm. The first and second graders who are making an imaginary television program about weather need to visit the studio at a local college of further education, where the staff and students help them gain the experience required to progress with their drama. Another class is halfway through the Nativity story before it occurs to us that none of the children actually knows what an inn is. . . . This time we just tell them.

Any extra experience the learners may need can come from us, from stories, from books, from pictures (to be studied and interpreted), from film and television, from radio, from visits to museums, visits to farms, visits anywhere, from parents and other adults, from any source of information available. All that is necessary is that they feel they have enough to start the drama happily. What they know may be very limited and, from an adult's point of view, distorted and inaccurate. That does not matter. They will build on their own collective experience and what they do not know between them they can guess. They can check the effectiveness of their guessing afterwards. It is one of the virtues of Drama that it motivates learners to hypothesize, imagine, experiment, and explore, and then to research so that they can test the validity of whatever they have come up with. They are acquiring that most essential and perhaps one of the rarest of all educational resources—*the need to know.*

## 2. Creating a Context

The great strength of Drama as a learning medium is that it allows students to learn in the way that is most natural to them—in the context of situations and stories and happenings that they recognize as lifelike. They can readily involve themselves in these if the context is right, if it engages them. They are offered the opportunity to think, to feel, to talk, to act, and so to learn as they normally learn in the real world—through experience and in collaboration with others. This is more than cerebral, abstract learning; it is physical, particular learning. It is learning grounded in experience, learning that is not easily forgotten or ignored. One only has to watch the commitment, passion, and subtlety with which young players defend a fictional cause they have made their own in a drama to recognize the effectiveness of the medium as a context for learning.

### 3. Finding a Focus and Involving Everyone

However the students and their teacher arrive at it, a focus that concentrates and directs the energies of the learners is required for the drama to take off. As teachers, our job is to elicit as wide as possible a range of views, commitments, interests, and concerns as exists in the class—even before we start to provoke new ones. Moreover, we need to return to the differences once the drama is underway. But at the same time, if the class is to work together on this drama, then we have to focus and concentrate their attentions at certain moments. We want to involve and make space for everyone, but we have to work at holding the drama together at times. This pattern of widening out to take in as much as possible and narrowing down to create a focus is characteristic of the whole process. (See Figure 2.)

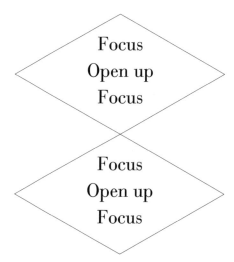

FIGURE 2. THE DOUBLE DIAMOND

Sometimes the focus will become clear after some initial explorations; perhaps various STILL IMAGES (see page 75) of bullying, for example, may lead to the class agreeing to focus on just one of these and develop it as their drama. (If possible, ideas from the other STILL IMAGES may be incorporated as work progresses. If people invest time and energy creating even something as simple as a STILL IMAGES they may be reluctant to abandon it altogether.)

An easier, though less dramatically engaging, approach to the focal starting point may be simply to brainstorm an issue and, by general agreement, to select a focus from the range of suggestions.

Often the teacher will determine the focus with an initial stimulus that seems likely to work with this class.

Example:

Teacher [*To Year Seven students, having made it absolutely clear that they are engaging in a fiction*] A new pupil is joining us shortly and we should like your help in preparing for his arrival. His name is Matthew, and he gets about by means of a wheelchair. We suspect that the school will need some changes if Matthew is to move around freely and live, work, and play happily here. You know more about the ins and outs of the school than anyone. Would you be willing to draw up plans for whatever changes are necessary?

This particular starting point led to some interesting revelations, one of which will be described shortly.

## 4. Building Belief

Once the commitment to a particular story or problem to be solved is given, then the building of belief is underway. What is called for is not total suspension of disbelief. In fact, belief is possibly a misleading word here. What is required is that we all agree to take seriously the fictional world we are starting to create. The importance of my commitment, as a teacher, is paramount. I do not have to be solemn or theatrical, but whether I am in role or out of role, observing or assisting, I have to take the work seriously, both the students' contributions and my own. More of that in a moment.

## 5. Cross-Curricular Gains

Having grounded the learning in a particular fictional context, having generated energy and focused it, and having established some preliminary commitment, the teacher now has the opportunity to range over the whole curriculum in considering where the drama might go next. By whole curriculum, of course, we mean the curriculum of perceived student needs as identified by teachers and schools, which is wider and richer than, though it may necessarily include, the national curriculum or other statutory requirements. While such subjects such as English and History most obviously offer areas for development through Drama, some of the possibilities across the curriculum are perhaps less self-evident, and a few examples may be useful.

## Writing

Even reluctant writers sometimes write with enthusiasm because their role as an evacuee or a litigant or a journalist or a bard demands that they do so. The drama supplies something to write about, and it can provide a shared experience in which to collaborate with other writers. It offers the easiest and most natural way, short of the real thing, of introducing a need for a variety of styles and registers of both speaking and writing for different purposes and in different contexts. On occasion it can even lead directly to the real thing. Another class of Liverpool students, several of whom actually were in wheelchairs, decided to write to a local cinema about access after exploring the issue in a drama.

## Mathematics

Math problems can take on a new significance if they arise in the context of planning the layout of a village or a canal or a zoo, or of working out quantities and resources for an expedition, or the finances of a business the class has carefully built up. One Liverpool teacher, now a headteacher, conducted her Math lessons for a year through simulations of a bank and its customers (see page 102).

## Personal and Social Education

The Year Seven classes that were preparing their school for the fictional Matthew in his wheelchair produced many practical schemes to this end. We were concerned, however, with shifting their thinking toward a critical reflection on their own school experience. What needs to be done to allow all of us to live, work, and play happily in this school? The most telling discovery came near the end of the four sessions.

Small groups are presenting images of situations they want to change, in a mode of FORUM THEATRE (see page 82). A group of four girls stand; they are clearly mocking a fifth girl who appears to be eating at a table.

CLASS [*Observing this*] Oh, yeah. She's finishing her dinner. So they're laughing at her.

TEACHERS [*Two class teachers and two advisory teachers, exchanging puzzled looks*] Sorry? Explain that, will you?

STUDENT [*Scornful of their ignorance*] If you finish your school dinner it means you're either a scav or you're so poor you don't have enough to eat at home. So they're laughing at her.

[*Pause*]

TEACHER [*Quietly*] How many of you wish you could finish your dinner at school?

The whole group, two Year Seven classes, slowly raise their hands—all of them. There is a silence while the significance of this sinks in. How many other unwritten and totally unwanted codes are young people like these eleven- and twelve-year-olds imposing on themselves? Drama is one way of making the invisible visible. It is a way of tackling, in the safety of fiction, certain personal and social issues that need to be addressed, issues such as this one and others, even more prevalent, such as bullying and juvenile power dressing.

### Other Subjects

Scientific investigation ("It's just like being a real scientist," confides one bright ten-year-old as she leaves at the end of a science fiction drama), having to speak a foreign language because the dramatic situation demands it, composing a piece of music in an attempt to communicate with an alien (an astonishing and impressive and unexpected outcome, this), mapping and map reading, orienteering, swimming, canoeing, mountaineering . . . the list of possible learning activities dealt with through the fictional context of Drama is endless.

The contexts can range from the exotic to the mundane; the learners can be framed as themselves or as fictional or historical characters; the time can be the past, the present, the future. The only essential is that the context engages the learners and what happens in the drama comes to matter to them—they believe in it and want to do something about it. The process of learning through Drama is underway.

### 6. Asking Questions

If our aim is to encourage the learners' control over the learning and to ensure their confidence in what they are doing, then we have to look carefully at the sort of questions we ask.

## Table 1.   Teacher's Questions

### Open Questions

*Real questions to which there may be many answers.*

*The purpose of such questions may be:*

| | |
|---|---|
| to seek information | What do you know about Travellers? |
| to stimulate thought | I wonder why you chose to be a Traveller? |
| to deepen insight | In whose interest is it that we should move on? |
| to encourage debate | What can we tell the councillors and locals? |
| to provoke decisions | What shall we do? |
| to focus on implications | Shall we see how they might react to this? |
| to elicit hypotheses | What is most likely to be their first response? |
| to motivate research | What do the (real) press cuttings suggest? |
| to encourage predictions | If we do what they ask what'll happen? |
| to prompt comparisons | Do other people get treated in this way? |
| to inspire empathy | I wonder how they felt? |
| to reveal emotions | So what are your feelings about this now? |
| to explore reactions | Do we have any right to behave this way? |
| to establish mood | I can't take any more. Is anyone else for quitting? |
| to shift a focus | What sort of homes do these locals have anyway? |
| to hold or regain attention | Has anyone heard what the police are up to? |
| to check understanding | Does anyone know about rights of way? |

### Other Kinds of Questions

*Less open perhaps, even closed or leading, but often helpful.*

*These may be used:*

| | |
|---|---|
| to control or direct | Shall I tell the press we'll prepare a statement? |
| to help overcome an impasse | Let's decide. Yes or no? |
| to avoid fantasy | Are we really likely to be armed to the teeth? |
| to supply clues | Did anyone notice the councillor snooping about? |
| to prompt | Would it help to elect a spokesperson? |
| to remind | Didn't we agree that we had no firearms? |
| to assist with problems | Are you willing to be responsible for this? |

60

The more that we can ask open questions (see Table 1) the better. Asking open questions, however, can create problems. We may ask an open question but really only want one answer. We feel that it is the obvious or the ideal answer, and in any case it is the only answer that will lead the lesson in the direction we have planned; we really cannot handle any other. We are playing the celebrated game of "guess what's in my head." In such circumstances it is surely more honest not to ask a question at all but to tell the class if there is something we want them to know, in order to make progress. Perhaps as teachers we ask too many questions. It's an occupational disease.

## 7. Honoring All Responses

What if we ask a genuinely open question and we get a genuinely silly answer, either because a child has misunderstood, misjudged, or is misbehaving? As a rule we must, if we can, honor all answers to an open question, at least to the extent of taking them as seriously as they have been offered. A brief supplementary question may be enough to allow the answerer to see the implications of a wildly inappropriate response, without wasting too much time and without making the answerer feel too silly. But what if the response appears to be a deliberate challenge? Is, say, racist or sexist? Then we have a choice. The simplest way out is to invite the offender to take his or her work seriously and behave; this school and this class have a policy that does not tolerate such conduct. Sometimes that is the obvious solution. But it may be far more useful to honor even the most offensive responses, for two reasons. One is that class jokers (assuming this is one) may be helped to take themselves more seriously if asked to take responsibility for their utterances. The second is that, taken seriously, the "joke" may surprise us all and lead to insights and enlightenment that we would never have reached if we had ignored or suppressed it. The following is an account of such an instance.

A thing* of bloodthirsty Vikings (eight-year-olds; two-thirds male) sit around the fire. Each is in role as a Sagaman, or storyteller. Each is also a warrior who cannot wait to sail out and pillage. They have been subjected to three weeks of delaying tactics by the Drama teacher, in self-inflicted role as a messenger (male) from Freja (goddess of peace and loving kindness), who has been commissioned by the class' own teacher to challenge the rampant

---

*It may seem strange, but this really is the collective noun for a gathering of Vikings. The *Compact Edition of the Oxford English Dictionary* has over two pages on the noun "thing," but this particular meaning is the first one it cites. It is apparently derived from the Old Norse for a meeting or council, and hence the more common meaning of the matter that has to be transacted by the assembly.

machismo of her young men. Not so easy under the circumstances. The hapless messenger tries one last, desperate throw.

MESSENGER OF FREJA [*Solemnly*] Perhaps we should not set out tomorrow. Perhaps some of us might want to stay behind.

FIRST WARRIOR [*He can hardly contain himself. He seizes the official rod that allows him to speak and fixes the messenger with a winning smile.*] I think the wimps should stay behind.

MESSENGER [*Half expecting a sexist foray and so mishearing*] You think the women should stay behind?

SECOND WARRIOR [*Beaming up at the* MESSENGER] No. He said "wimps"!

MESSENGER [*Trapped. Could this be the time to come out of role and talk firmly about taking our work seriously and . . . ? No. Trust the medium. Trust the principles. An open question was implied: Should anyone stay behind? Honor the question.*] Mm . . . I see. Wimps, eh. It's a difficult word, "wimps." I mean, who here would admit to being a wimp? [*That might shut him up for a minute.*]

THIRD WARRIOR [*The only black boy in the class*] I am a wimp. [*He stands with great dignity in a circle of awed silence. Does he realize what he has said? He is a bright lad. He clearly is aware of the significance, but can he carry it off?*]

MESSENGER Well. What a remarkable . . . what a bold thing for a Viking warrior to admit! Can you tell us why you said this?

THIRD WARRIOR [*A brief pause while he thinks*] No.

MESSENGER Okay. Everyone—thought track him. What could have made him say this? Why might a Viking admit to being a wimp? [*Help!*]

VIKING WOMAN He is a wimp and he's proud of it because he doesn't have to show off all the time so he's got lots of friends.

She is talking about the boy more than about Vikings but the simple force of her observation is not lost on the class. Three more wimps (all males) suddenly volunteer themselves. The four of them remain behind to plan defenses for the village. But what is even more interesting is the nature of the pillage that follows.

One small group of Vikings is actually defeated. Another group becomes Anglo-Saxon and depicts the consequences of pillage from the receiving end. The level of seriousness and reflection has shifted dramatically.

The challenge to machismo has finally come from within the class, from within the drama, and the students, while still having fun, are seriously facing some of the implications of their decisions and actions. They are taking stock of their values.

In this instance, the ridiculing of wimps was perhaps less serious than an overtly sexist or racist interjection might have been, but it did reflect a somewhat aggressive insecurity of the sort the class teacher was concerned about.

Arguably, the most important struggle in the world today is the struggle to accept and deal with difference: difference of style, culture, class, gender, sexuality, race, nationality, creed, ability—difference from any norm imposed by fear and intolerance. For teachers it poses the question of whether to attempt to outlaw bigotry and oppression when they manifest themselves in our classrooms, or whether to tackle them by facing them. If we try the latter tack, we may be able to expose them for what they are. We may be able to analyze and define them. We may be able to reveal their roots and their seeds. We can challenge them. Moreover, we can attempt to construct lessons designed to do all those things. In the end, we may help to make it more difficult to dismiss another human being simply for being too different—or sometimes too alike—for comfort.

## 8. Active and Interactive Techniques

Finally, to complete the Ring of Confidence, a range of techniques or conventions for shaping their dramas is at the learners' disposal. Some examples of these can be found on pages 72–73. A useful checklist of the most common conventions can be found in Jonothan Neelands' *Structuring Drama Work* (1990). And teachers and pupils will always adapt and devise new techniques for themselves.

## 9. Reflection: Making the Process and Purpose Explicit

At some stage, preferably sooner rather than later, the learners should understand quite clearly what they are being asked to engage in and why. Drama is not simply about having fun; it is creating a forum for learning. The participants should know that and should be aware of the nature of the learning as soon as they are capable of doing so. If a drama about survival on a desert island is intended as a metaphor by which to explore concepts such as cooperation, conflict, and responsibility in society in general and in their own lives in particular, then the learners may just benefit from being told that; otherwise, as discovered by researchers Edwards and Mercer, they might arrive at a very different understanding of intended outcomes. The pupils discussed in Edwards and Mercer's study *Common Knowledge* (1987;

pages 53–54), were age seven and eight. They were asked what they thought their drama had been all about, what they had learned, and what they thought their teacher hoped they would get from what they had done. The sort of answers they gave were:

JOANNE It teaches you about what would really happen if you were on a desert island, what it's like on a desert island.

ANGELINA [*After a few moments' hesitation*] I would think that I would learn I would never go on a boat again.

As with any experiential learning process, room must be made in Drama for reflection and analysis if the full learning potential is to be realized. This can happen

- while still in role, within the drama;
- by stopping the drama to discuss what is happening and make sense of it in terms of our own experience and vice versa;
- by engaging in an activity such as drawing or writing or some other marking of a moment from the drama that allows for reflection and analysis.

## *10. Empowering the Learners . . . As Artists*

The ultimate aim of this model of Educational Drama is to give power and responsibility and control in learning to learners who are working in the medium of an art form, who are learning as artists. The manifold skills of the actor, designer, director, choreographer, playwright, may all be evident in any classroom drama, often to a high degree, even early in a class' development. We live in a society where from the earliest age we are exposed to a variety of forms of Drama, mainly on television, but also on radio, in the cinema, and at the theatre. Raymond Williams has called ours a dramatized society. He argues that "Drama, in quite new ways, is built into the rhythms of everyday life. . . . In earlier periods Drama was important at a festival, in a season, or as a conscious journey to a theatre; from honoring Dionysus or Christ to taking in a show. What we now have is Drama as habitual experience; more in a week, in many cases, than most human beings would previously have seen in a lifetime." (*Writing in Society* [1983], page 12)

There are, moreover, simple everyday cultural practices that inform our dramatic techniques, telling stories, telling jokes, adopting roles, exploiting body language. All of us, students and teachers, have absorbed an enormous amount about the art of Drama. The realization, exploration, and development of that implicit knowledge is what is going on as we teach and learn through the art form in our classrooms.

# — PART TWO —
# THE PROCESS

Having considered some basic principles about how to manage a Drama in safety that conclude with the stated aim of empowering our learners as artists, we now need to think about what we really mean by that. What sort of learning do we have in mind? What exactly do we mean by "artists?" In a word, why are we working this way?

What follows is the outline of a set of awarenesses that informs our thinking as we work with learners of all ages. Other teachers may well have a different set because their educational priorities are different, but the issues raised in this section have to be addressed in one way or another.

## A BALANCE OF AWARENESSES

There are three areas of awareness that we cannot avoid attending to. They are the management of:

Content
Form
People

At times, your attention on all three of these areas of awareness may coincide in perfect balance, the drama may be uncovering truths in an

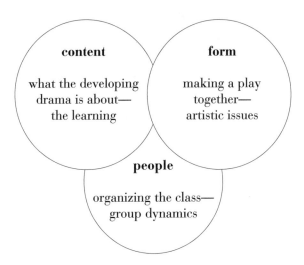

**content**

what the developing drama is about— the learning

**form**

making a play together— artistic issues

**people**

organizing the class— group dynamics

FIGURE 3. CONTENT, FORM AND PEOPLE

DRAMA AS A CONTEXT FOR LEARNING: PUPILS FROM SPEKE PRIMARY
SCHOOLS AND SPEKE COMMUNITY COMPREHENSIVE WORK TOGETHER IN
SPEKE HALL AS "TIME DETECTIVES" ON A PROJECT INVOLVING HISTORY,
MATHEMATICS, INFORMATION TECHNOLOGY, AND PERSONAL AND SOCIAL
EDUCATION.

artistically satisfying way, and the whole class may be involved and learning to the top of its bent. This would be the ideal situation. But on occasions you may need to concentrate on one or two areas at the temporary expense of the third. What happens if a small group is developing something interesting and you feel that in terms of both content and form it is worthy of all your attention?

## PEOPLE: ORGANIZING THE CLASS

A focused activity with one small group may leave the rest of the class less than fully involved for a short time. They may be in role as audience. As long as they are happy with that role and benefitting from watching, that is fine, but there is more they can do.

Augusto Boal (1992; page xxiv) talks about spectators becoming "spect-actors." If we take his hint, our class can be encouraged to join in the drama it is watching by suggesting ideas, dialogue, direction, thoughts for the central characters, sound effects, and any other refinements that, if accepted, may enhance the drama and expand the ownership. Individual spect-actors may get up and replace existing actors or become additional actors if the original creators of the scene agree.

Throughout the "Teacher's Tool Kit" there are suggestions as to how activities may be varied and involvement sustained as the lesson moves from whole class to small group work, to paired tasks, and back again.

The single most important thought that holds all this together and informs all our planning is the awareness of the collaborative nature of the theatrical process. We are *always* working together to explore through the drama whatever it is that we, as a class, can learn from the events. Some people may sometimes seem to have an awful lot more to offer than others, but their work is always only a part of our work and is always simply their contribution to what we are all learning.

So what is it that we are learning—in terms of content first?

## CONTENT: WHAT THE DEVELOPING DRAMA IS ABOUT

We have said that Drama has to do with trying to make sense of the world. So far we have presented this within the context of learning about the world through the subjects generally taught in schools. We have talked about English and History and Math and Personal and Social Education and the other areas of what we call the curriculum. But what is it exactly that we are trying to do with our drama in these designated areas? What sort of learning is Drama best suited for?

Drama represents a way of organizing experience by creating heightened
awareness through the play of language and gesture.

BRIAN WATKINS*

"Heightened awareness"—it sounds intriguing. How do I get that in my
classroom? Where is the National Curriculum document that offers that as a
target. Not in so many words, maybe, but what sort of awarenesses might we
be talking about, and could we locate them in programs of study we are
already committed to?

Could these awarenesses be something like the following?

- Awareness of why we do what we do:
  Personally why, historically why, socially why, culturally why, politically why;
- Awareness of what makes us the way we are:
  All those forces, personal, social, historical, etc., that go into shaping
  who we are;
- Awareness of the implications of what we do:
  The cost of the choices we make and the decisions we take;
- Awareness of how the world works:
  In whatever situation we have chosen to look at: Who is in control?
  Whose interests are being served? Whose interests are not being
  served?

In all these moments of heightened awareness we would be trying to
uncover insights and understandings that might help us to make sense of
things, things on the curriculum, things that matter to our lives. We would
be looking for things to celebrate and build on and things to question and
change. We would be looking for contradictions and confusions that take
hold when people are unaware. We would be working to make the invisible
visible so that we are in a position to do something about it. The pupils
described on page 58—59, who uncovered the truth that they would all like
to finish their dinners but had all been responsible for ensuring that not one
of them did, had achieved a heightened awareness. They learned through
their drama.

As teachers, we can always be alert to the possibilities of helping the
class to achieve such moments of heightened awareness. As learners, the
class needs to know (as soon as they are capable of realizing what it means)
that through their Drama work they can do this.

So, in developing a drama, who is responsible for what? What role has
the teacher? What role have the learners?

*In "Drama," in *Making Language Work* (1981), page 209.

## The Children's Role

- To play;
- To believe in the play;
- To make decisions;
- To reflect on their actions;
- To listen to each other;
- To take both themselves and each other seriously:
  - What is it that they want to say?
  - What stories do they want to tell?
  - What voices are they finding?
  - What different visions are they forging?
- To discover things for themselves by making the invisible visible;
- And last but by no means least, an important part of their role must be to appreciate, to enjoy, and to make the most of the art form of theatre (Drama).

## The Teacher's Role

- To help get things started;
- To help focus on a moment or an image from which drama can grow;
- To help sustain belief in the fiction;
- To help structure what happens:
  - so that the many voices can all be heard;
  - so that those quiet or tentative voices which might get lost are assured a hearing;
  - so that a variety of dramatic conventions is made available to them;
  - so that the unpredictable is there to surprise and intrigue them;
- To look and listen;
- To introduce tensions and challenges:
  - so that the drama can expose dilemmas and contradictions;
  - so that significant questions are being asked;
  - so that the invisible can be made visible;
- And last but by no means least, an important part of our role must be to help formulate artistic criteria that will make for satisfying drama.

# FORM: WHAT ARTISTIC CRITERIA MIGHT APPLY

Once again we are talking about a set of awarenesses rather than rules. Both teacher and learners are bringing to their work at the very least an intuitive sense of form, culled from living in a "dramatized society." Provided the result is not an ossified set of rules, it cannot but help to attempt, at times, to articulate these intuitions and use them consciously to shape or reshape what we are doing.

What follows is a list of suggestions. They are deliberately phrased as questions in order to stress the point that artistic criteria cannot be fixed and immutable. Some principles may seem pretty unarguable and some of the questions a little less than open, but in art the hope of establishing hard and fast rules is always fanciful so the questions are genuinely questions.

- Focusing on the particular. Is specific detail usually more suggestive and effective and revealing than generalized action or gestures? Sovereigns can indicate their sovereignty by sitting on their thrones generally looking haughty, or they can be doing something more specific, such as signing a document (even while shaving) that might lead to the siege and destruction of a certain city. Where might this be taking place? In a tent, in a boot-churned field? The detail starts to bring a vague image of sovereignty into focus, starts to make it physical, starts to bring it to life.
- Showing rather than telling. Wherever possible, can we trust the dramatic process and create the moment rather than talk about it? Show it and then talk about it afterwards, maybe?
- Economy of style. In the theatre they have a saying, "Less is more." Is our drama likely to be clearer, more incisive, more powerful and therefore more effective if we concentrate on cutting things down to a minimum whenever we can?
- Slowing things down. Less may mean more, but can we give due attention to the less, can we avoid rushing it? Can we develop a rhythm of working that allows us to take our time over what we are constructing, a measured rhythm that creates space for things to happen in, allowing us to reflect and concentrate?
- Suggesting rather than asserting. Can we let the audience (the spect-actors, our classmates) do the thinking when we show them something? If we do, is it possible that what we are trying to reveal or say may be that much richer than if we spell it out too plainly?
- Attention to significant structural elements of drama. Would our work benefit from a conscious attempt to control and make more effective our use of some of the following?
  - space and how we deploy ourselves in it
  - forms and intensity of sound
  - silence
  - pace     • timing
  - rhythms of speech and movement

- tension: when the drama starts to bite, something is being revealed, awareness is heightened
- relaxation
- energy
- physicality
- movement
- stillness

The search for effective artistic form in drama might be pursued by attending to the variety and contrast, the similarities and echoes, the juxta-positions and disruptions within and between these elements. They are the elements of performance that, whether consciously or unconsciously, every actor and director must take into account. They are how we realize whatever it is we are trying to realize "on stage." Much of our skill in using them, in the theatre and in the classroom, is intuitive. If we articulate and sometimes expressly concentrate on them, if we make our awareness of their availability more explicit, we may be able to make our work and our children's work more telling and more satisfying.

It may have escaped the notice of my class that to attract attention, still-ness and silence can sometimes work more dramatically than sound and fury. If I point it out, at an appropriate stage in a drama, I am offering an additional skill for their repertoire.

Other awarenesses that might be useful to have at the back of our minds while we are helping our pupils to shape their dramas are the effec-tiveness of:

- Dramatic irony. For example, in an improvised confrontation between two people, revealing and ironic effects can be achieved by having two other players voice the secret thoughts of the speakers (over their shoulders) at appropriate moments in the dialogue.
- Juxtaposing contrasting images and events. Are we learning to see the dramatic potential of structuring our work so that the whole says more than the discrete parts?
- Suspense. Constraints, frustrations, and delay have to be built into the process, often by the teacher in role, but as the students develop the skill they too can exploit this essential element of the playwright's craft.
- The unexpected. On occasions, it may be worth making a conscious effort to avoid the predictable, the obvious, the normal.
- The inevitable. Oh, yes, we saw that coming.
- Emphasis. Can you say that, or do that, again, but make it stand out? How might you mark this moment, make it more significant?
- Repetition. Occasionally it pays to repeat a word or a statement or a question. Words can have a physical effect on us. They play on our

nerve ends. Remember Laurence Olivier in *The Marathon Man*—"Is it safe? Is it safe?"

- Understatement. Which can sometimes move us more powerfully than overassertion would.
- The unspoken. The silence that can be even more telling still.
- Stylization. Play it for effect.
- Alienation. Play it strange; hold it at arm's length to be judged.
- Naturalism. Play it real.
- Caricature. Play it for laughs. (But beware! It can undermine and lead to an avoidance of all seriousness).
- Symbolism. Not easy to agree on a simple definition of this. Gavin Bolton (1992, p. 43) suggests it has to do with the accretion of meaning around a sign. John O'Toole (1992, p. 220) links it to Drama resonating with reality. In the Conwy Castle drama (page 133), when Edward ordered the Welsh tribes to hand over their banners and insignia (which the children had made themselves and had proudly borne throughout) and then threw them onto the muddy ground, the symbolic significance of that final crude act of dismissal struck home at more than one level. In a sense it was a really mean thing for a teacher to do to children's handiwork, but that very meanness contributed to its effect as a *coup de theatre*, and it certainly worked.
- Ritual. Can be useful in the early stages of drama as a means of building commitment and belief; can lend weight or ceremony to an occasion. Taking another tack, can our dramas expose and challenge the ways in which ritual is used formally and informally in our everyday lives? Are these sorts of behavior necessary, natural, normal? Is *any* form of human behavior inevitable?
- Music, song, chant, incantation, verse. Perhaps all of these can enhance dramatic exploration as much as they do dramatic performance.

and of course, last but not least

- Humor.

It goes without saying that a set of awarenesses such as this is not a checklist any more than it is a set of rules. In planning and working on a drama no teacher and no class is going to try to incorporate all of the above. But both in planning and in execution, some of these considerations will be of use at some time.

# — PART THREE —
# TECHNIQUES

What follows is a brief outline of a number of techniques for structuring Drama work.

## TEACHER IN ROLE

This is a particularly useful technique, as it allows teachers both to be involved in the drama and to structure it. It is important that teachers choose their roles sensitively, so that by definition their status does not over-whelm student responses. It is therefore useful to choose a low-status role if possible (e.g., alien or stranger) or a high-status one where the character has a problem (e.g., a lion lacking courage, a giant with a toothache).

Within this strategy this character's difficulties become the focus for the dramatic starting point. Drama is necessarily about a *perceived crisis*, how-ever small or however threatening.

Example:

Fellow astronauts, we have traveled back in time to the planet of our forebears, Earth. Let us see for ourselves the events that caused Earth's destruction and perhaps change the course of history.

A caveat. While referring to history, we should mention that people sometimes worry about Drama's supposed tinkering with historical fact. Let us be quite clear: Educational Drama deals with fictions. In History through Drama, all we can ask is what might have happened when . . . , or why things might have happened, or how. We can only make hypotheses. But these guesses might then prompt us to research; they might stimulate us and provide us with the need to find out more. This is the main bequest that Drama offers History. It creates a context for inquiry, for empathy and understanding and it helps children to become real historians, eager to find out what they need to know.

## MANTLE OF THE EXPERT

This is the other side of the **TEACHER IN ROLE** equation. If the teacher, in role, has a problem, then the dynamic of the lesson requires that the students operate within a context that allows them to come up with solutions. **MANTLE OF THE EXPERT** creates such a context. With this technique the teacher signals that the children have all the knowledge and expertise to deal with the situa-tion. Whether they really have or not, the game allows them to play as though they had, which encourages them to contribute actively and with confidence to the drama and to their learning within it.

Example:

TEACHER I was just walking through the market when I saw this package on the floor. I went up to it and heard it ticking, so I called you people. You're the bomb disposal experts; what are you going to do now?

Or the approach might be less demanding, more low key:

Example:

TEACHER I'm a student who's just arrived in this school. What do I need to know about it?

## STILL IMAGE

Sometimes called "tableau" or "freeze frame," this is a way of focusing on a specific moment. As it is such a deliberate and formal procedure, it requires participants to become aware of subtleties of positioning, body language, and relationships. They have to choose with care the precise moment that captures just what they want to convey in their tableaux. Inexperienced students should be introduced to it carefully.

Model an image in the middle, adding one person at a time, until the whole class is clear how an image works. Sculpting other people may make the exercise easier and involve more of the class in this initial activity. Working from a photograph or a picture can also help sometimes.

Having set up and held the moment, which is without movement or dialogue, having discussed and interpreted it, perhaps having refined and improved it, with the help of the whole class, we are then in a position to work around the image if we wish. We can simply add a caption or we can introduce other strategies such as THOUGHT TRACKING, VIDEO TRACKING, and IMPROVISATION and thus bring the STILL IMAGE to life.

## THOUGHT TRACKING

What is this character thinking at this moment?

This is an invaluable technique for involving the whole class while they are watching an activity or a STILL IMAGE in the middle. It can often provide a rich seam of insights into what is going on at any time. And because contradictory thoughts are often presented by different people in the group, the final texture of the character's thinking may be far more complex and interesting and true to life than the ideas provided by the one individual playing the role.

WITHIN A STILL IMAGE, PUPILS CAN BE MATERIAL OBJECTS AS WELL AS
PEOPLE. HERE A "QUEEN" SITS ON HER THRONE WITH "CARVED DOGS"
ON THE ARMRESTS AND "LAP DOGS" AT HER SIDES.

## VIDEO TRACKING

Once confidence has been established in setting up **STILL IMAGES,** try moving one forward, referring to video format. "Run" the scene for a few seconds and "pause" it again. When participants become more confident, they can **IMPROVISE** for longer periods. If appropriate, the teacher can "fast forward" the scene in time, or "rewind" to other moments or **STILL IMAGES.** The rest of the class can be actively involved in this process by suggesting thoughts, dispositions, and dialogue for the characters.

Example:

Start with a **STILL IMAGE** of an incident of bullying or a fight. Use this format to investigate the thoughts and motivations of the bully and/or other participants. Analyze the situation, its antecedents and consequences, using the spectators to comment on and inform the process. Then focus on ways of refining and improving what has been created. It may well be that the other characters, parents, teachers, friends, have to be introduced, consulted, and involved, but eventually, the scene(s) can be "rewound" and "replayed," refined and changed, and this fictional representation and exploration of a problem may then be applied and referred to real life strategies for dealing with bullying and violence.

## IMPROVISATION

This generally means acting out a situation without previous planning or structuring. There is likely to be an element of improvisation in most classroom drama. Indeed, encouraged by exam boards, some secondary classroom dramas have consisted of little else. The problem with this is that, although many youngsters are ingenious improvisers and spontaneous improvisation can be great fun, there are limitations to its value. For example:

- Sustaining an improvisation creatively is difficult.
- Building in depth and challenge is even more difficult.
- Resisting the temptation to play for laughs, especially if performing to an audience, is almost impossible.
- What is also impossible—though often attempted—is improvising at some length and then, when it is your turn, trying to recreate the same for an audience.*

*What generally happens is that an approximation of the original, but lacking the original's spontaneity and conviction, is cobbled together. It has to be said that, inspired by the roar of the greasepaint, some more experienced performers can successfully create what is in effect a new piece out of the old. But to be successful in this way the entertainment value of what the

- Furthermore, improvised sketches, done in small groups, are likely to be fragmented and without any context.
- When showing one unrelated (though often thematically identical) sketch after another, it is hard to avoid competition or disillusion and disaffection. Educational Drama is, and must be, essentially a collaborative art and that is one of its greatest strengths.

All this said, however, improvisation *as an element of the work* is the central, and often the most enjoyable, technique at our students' disposal.

Improvisation may most commonly be used by the Teacher in Role interacting with:

- the whole class in role;
- individuals in role;

which interaction, in turn, may be:

- centrally focused with all others observing;
- in the midst of a class busy about its own improvisations. The teacher moves among the whole group, engaging one or two at a time in improvised dialogue, while the others continue with their own activities.

Improvisation may be also used by the teacher out of role guiding VIDEO TRACKING from STILL IMAGES.

It may also be used by small groups who:

- report back to a MEETING, rather than recreate, what their improvisation has revealed;
- answer the teacher's questions (such as "Did anyone have difficulties with the animals today? There seemed to be some disturbance in the lions' cage. . . .") and a new improvised dialogue is underway, building on and developing the original;
- learn to structure what they have improvised, possibly around key images, in order to present it to others. In this way they learn to avoid the impossible challenge of trying to reproduce exactly, in front of an audience, what they have just spontaneously and inimitably improvised without an audience. (See page 39, on performing for other people.)

---

Americans call the "skit" has to be high, and one is forced to ask: At what cost? Stereotypes, stock responses, and worse—racism, sexism, and ageism—are sometimes presented, and there is no inherent mechanism for challenging them. The best a teacher can do is intervene to stop the drama.

## TIME OUT

When a short scene is being played out by a small number of characters, TIME OUT is a useful ploy for involving the spectators. The teacher simply stops the action and the characters attach themselves to groups of people around them for advice and support. It may not be feasible for the advisers to come up with a script, but they can suggest ideas and possible lines of approach to adopt when the action is resumed.

## CALLING A MEETING

It is often useful, whatever the context, to call a MEETING as part of the action, to clarify and reflect on what is happening and to negotiate ways forward.

## FRAMING

This refers to the overall situation that students (and teacher) adopt in any drama. Whether they are to be framed as EXPERTS or not, it is important that all are clear about who they are. Do you want to frame them as Viking villagers, or would it be better with this class to frame them as modern historians or museum curators investigating Viking village life? The historians/curators can then recreate moments of village life to be studied and discussed. In this way, the students are moving from one frame to another.

Even if students are framed as students, it is essential that they recognize they are all in role.

- They must be free to try out uncharacteristic stances if they wish.
- They must be free from any fear of being personally mocked for the way they look, what they do or what they say (see page 33).

## ROLE ON THE WALL

In setting up a drama it is often important to establish and reflect on characters. ROLE ON THE WALL is a vivid means of transforming an "outline" character into a complex one. It provides a visual aid that can be built up by the students and is a useful reference point for dramatic development. It is a holding form for information that otherwise might get forgotten in the business of the drama.

This is a flavor of how it can work:

- First of all, draw a large "gingerbread" outline.
- Within the outline, put some agreed facts or ideas about the character. With younger children these can often be represented visually, for example, "happy" by a smiling face.

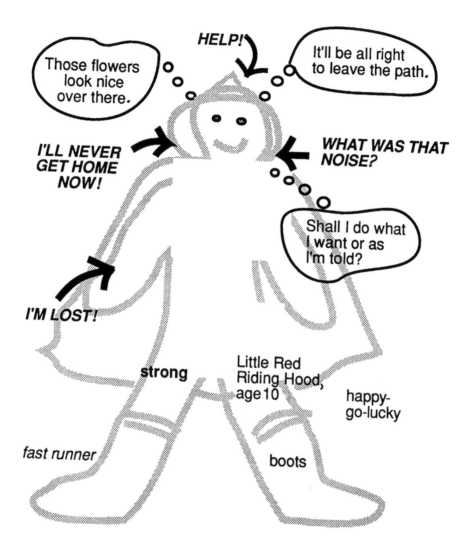

- As the character builds up or progresses through the story, additional qualities, attributes, clothing, even thoughts, can be written or drawn, to remain as a point of reference that will be useful to the class.
- Pressures can be applied to the character as tension mounts.
- Adapt this strategy to record, reflect on, and refine the character.

## NARRATIVE

As a linking and structuring device, narrative can be used, though sparingly, by the teacher, who watches the way that the students' play is progressing and sees that it needs direction or focusing or moving on. Similarly, students themselves can learn to use narrative, on occasions, to structure and advance a plot.

It may stand on its own or be an invitation to the class to mime or act out what is being narrated.

Example of simple narration:

After several weeks the scientists were no nearer to a solution so they decided to call in . . . [*Out of role for a moment*] Okay, so whom could we usefully call in here?

Example of narration with mime:

So all the parents of Hamelin made their way to the hill and in silence they sat facing the blank rock into which the stranger had led their children. . . .

## NARRATED ACTION

A different use of narration is as a mechanism to slow down and highlight and make strange, by stylizing, a particular moment in a drama. Characters in turn describe their interventions in the scene just before making them, doing so in the third person though talking about themselves.

Example:

HARRIET TUBMAN The woman takes her seat. [*She does so.*]

CONDUCTOR The conductor of the train faces the black passenger [*He turns and does so*], stares at her for a moment, then striding toward her he raises his voice and says, "You have no right to be on this train, woman. . . ."

PASSENGER NEAR BACK This woman turns to see what is happening. . . .

## SLOW MOTION

A useful controlling strategy if group action, especially whole class, needs to be contained, focused, made more precise, made strange. Examples of such action are running, bustling, and struggling activities; or using a tool, implement, or piece of machinery. (See page 37 on preventing students from becoming too involved.)

## FORUM THEATRE

The creation and recreation of an episode either through STILL IMAGES or through acting out, perhaps with the addition of THOUGHT TRACKING at critical moments—"Can we just freeze it there? What is this person thinking?" This enables a group to offer what they have done for reflection and for analysis by the rest of the class, who can suggest ways of changing and improving the situation. New players can, if they are willing, take over the original roles and play out their solutions to the problems raised by the first presenters of the scene.

Alternatively, groups of spectators can advise the characters on what they might say or do as the events change. The actors may want to call TIME OUT to consult those advisers or they may ask for a THOUGHT TRACK to base their next move on.

## HOT SEATING

Allows the whole class to engage in the exploration of a character's motives, values, behavior. The roleplayer is invited to sit in the middle while the rest of the class questions her about her actions and anything else that is deemed relevant.

## TWILIGHTING

Sometimes it may seem necessary to move into a drama gradually, to prepare the ground, to spend some time in the twilight zone between reality and the drama. One or two examples of this sort of activity appear elsewhere:

- Discussing a picture in order to build up a sense of place or time or character (see page 20)
- Using ROLE ON THE WALL to build up a character (see page 80)

Other simple examples of twilighting are:

- Asking what is already known about the subject to be dramatized
- Gradually building up the character of the teacher's role in the light of what might make the drama most interesting. This is almost the same as ROLE ON THE WALL, but the focus is directly on the teacher, who may adopt some props or articles of clothing, one at a time, as visual clues or stimuli to prompt the class' imagination. When the role is sufficiently established, the drama can get under way. The teacher, in role, is ready to present the problem or dilemma that the drama is to be about.
- Taking the students back in time. If a sense of what there was and wasn't in, say, the seventeenth century is evading the class, then a useful twilight exercise is the then and now game. In pairs, one child

mimes a simple twentieth-century activity for her partner. She has to think of the nearest seventeenth-century equivalent and mime that. So switching on a light might prompt lighting a candle in return. Turning on a television might suggest a minstrel or town crier. They take turns setting up the twentieth-century challenge and finding a seventeenth-century reply. Once confident of the process, a whole class can pair off and work simultaneously at this exercise for several minutes. If there is time, and if it seems profitable, a few pairs might be asked to show the others a sample or two to facilitate a brief discussion on what there was and what there wasn't in seventeenth-century England or America.

## GAMES AND EXERCISES

### 1. Warm-Ups

Actors in the theatre use what are sometimes called warm-up games and exercises to generate energy and to promote concentration, group awareness, responsiveness, and cohesion. Any of these objectives may be important for a particular class embarking on a drama or in the middle of a drama and encountering difficulties working together (see page 68 on developing the drama). One or two examples of the countless number available are:

- mirror games, in which mimes are mirrored by another or others;
- trust games, in which individuals rely on others to stop them from falling, or, with eyes closed, from bumping into others;
- socialized games that permit and encourage people to make physical contact, change habitual groupings, and cooperate with others in an atmosphere of fun and security. Parachutes for cooperative play come in handy here. But a host of circle games need no more than people and a willingness to relax and join in. They range from the energetic to the calming and should perhaps only be used when a particular need arises or when a group has earned a break from more concentrated, deliberative work, and physical release would do it good.

### 2. Games as an Integral Part of a Drama

Some games, as well as being useful for warm-up purposes, function well as a technique within a drama. The hand squeeze that travels round a circle can create a ritualized signal that the class is traveling through time, for example, until the squeeze has sped three times around, when we shall have arrived in the sixteenth century. The keeper of the keys game might serve as an initiative test to decide who has the skill to enter the dragon's den. A blindfolded player sits with a large bunch of keys in her lap and, with a rolled-up newspaper for a baton, attempts to strike a second player who has stealthily crept up to try and capture the keys undetected. The others watch until their turn comes.

One game that is really designed to help a group work spontaneously and sensitively together but has potential as an integral drama strategy as well is worth describing in some detail. The rules are simple and must be adhered to (except with very young children, perhaps). Only the leader can speak (great for a noisy class!) and no one is allowed to guide or direct anyone else. In other words, all responses must arise out of watching what everyone else does and deciding when to take the initiative and when to follow. The leader (initially the teacher, but soon others can take this role) says something like: "Can the group make one (group-sized) letter $O$ to the count of ten? One, two, three . . . [*The students simply stand in a circle.*] Can you make a capital $Q$? A capital $X$? Etc."

If by the count of ten the group isn't happy with what it has achieved, there's nothing to stop them having another go, starting again, but still without directing or negotiating of any sort.

After some successful attempts at shaping letters, the content can become more imaginative. "Can the group create a children's playground by the count of ten? Or a building site? Or a beach? Or an orchestra?" Or whatever the leader (who by this time might be one of the students) can think of?

Some of the pictures they create may be worth challenging. "Are you happy with this orchestra? It has five conductors and no wind instruments." If they are happy, that is fine. It is their creation. Chances are, though, that they will want a more balanced orchestra and at a second go they will really be watching each other and learning to react more sensitively. It is a moving thing to see a natural leader yield the baton to a normally less dominant friend. They are learning the art of ensemble playing.

The advantage of this exercise, of course, is that it frees the group to build images together without having time to worry. The urgency of having to complete the task by the count of ten paradoxically makes things easier. Energy is released and spontaneity and fun arise naturally. The exercise also creates an opportunity to reflect on the key concepts of energy, control, and cooperation. What sort of energy level are we operating at? How far have we got it in control? How well are we working together? How aware of and responsive to each other are we? Are we affirming or blocking each other's ideas? Asked sincerely and not as implied criticism or a put-down, these are questions that can lead a class to take responsibility for the key concepts and for their own behavior in a Drama lesson. Recognition and acceptance of the

AFRICAN DRUM MUSIC ACCOMPANIES A RITUAL DANCE THAT HAS BEEN DEVISED OUT OF A DRAMATIC NARRATIVE.

artistic disciplines that allow their work to happen can replace their need for teacher-imposed discipline, with a lot less stress for everyone.

This sort of game, perhaps accompanied by a discussion of artistic discipline, may be useful when introducing Drama to a group for the first time, or as a reminder part way through a course, or occasionally simply to spur a group into quick creation of a scenario during a particular Drama session.

# Act Four

# FORMULATING A SCHOOL DRAMA POLICY

## DRAMA'S PLACE IN THE CURRICULUM

Drama has an essential place in a broad and balanced curriculum.

## DRAMA AS AN ART FORM AND A TEACHING METHOD

The school development plan is at the heart of curricular and inservice planning and resource allocation. Drama should therefore be acknowledged in the development plan as a separate subject and/or part of the school's overall arts provision and as a way of teaching across subject areas. Because Drama is an art form it will benefit from close, creative interaction with the other arts in order to create a strong arts community within the school, but links must also be made with other subject areas so that Drama can support and resource them and vice versa. Drama should be recognized as a means of teaching a whole range of activities throughout the curriculum. It is a way of making sense of the world.

## DRAMA AS A CURRICULUM AND COMMUNITY RESOURCE

Drama's contribution to the school and its wider community is vital. It is a superb vehicle in areas such as Equal Opportunities (race and gender),

IN A CIRCLE A VIKING EXPEDITIONARY FORCE PAUSES TO REFLECT ON ITS HOPES AND EXPECTATIONS FOR THE COMING JOURNEY.

Parent-School Partnerships, Cross-phase Liaison (a liaison between elementary and high schools and Special Needs schools), school assemblies, and Special Needs. Schools can also be centers for community performances; in the United Kingdom, Regional Arts Boards have a policy of funding schools for arts initiatives of this kind.

## DRAMA RESOURCES

### 1. Space

Drama in Education can take place in and out of the school—from the most confined classroom to the grandest medieval castle to any kind of historical building.

### 2. Equipment

A suitable range of storybooks, poems, media texts (including television programs), photographs, works of art, toys, educational equipment from all curricular areas, and displays, reflecting the cultural diversity of our work, will provide invaluable stimuli and resource materials. A library of playscripts may also be useful, but a script requires time and care to bring it alive.

Books, information packs, and other such resources should be available for ongoing research once a drama is underway. Audio and video equipment can be used as a stimulus and for recording and assessing drama work.

Performance technology is available at a range of prices and levels. Schools must make their own decisions about what is most appropriate to their needs. For performances, blackout and a lighting system, as well as a sound system incorporating microphones, cassette deck, mixer, and loud-speakers are advisable. Materials for set and costume design and construction may also be considered.

## 3. Outside Bodies

Visits to theatres and performances by visiting companies are an important resource. Preparation and follow-up work is the key to gaining the maximum benefit from the experience. Backstage tours can be arranged. Local theatres, as part of their outreach programs, often send actors, directors, and technicians into schools to talk about their work.

Funding for theatre visits may come from two sources. Principals, with the endorsement of the governing bodies, can earmark monies from the school's annual budget toward the cost. In certain circumstances, schools can ask parents for voluntary contributions. Museums, historic buildings, art galleries, etc., are often keen to accommodate Drama projects and activities within their buildings.

The organizations' education departments should be contacted to negotiate the possibilities.

# Act Five

# DRAMA IN ACTION

## PRETEND CORNERS

### 1. Building from Experience

It is important that any "pretend corner" that is set up by students and teachers contain props and symbols that the children know, relate to, and understand (see Figure 1, The Ring of Confidence, page 55). For example, a "hospital" with stethoscopes, plastic syringes, blood pressure monitors, etc., may be less appropriate to the students' experiences than a more "low-key" health center. We need to ensure that the paraphernalia of the scene does not alienate the children from the issue in question, e.g., What happens when you're sick? Use techniques like ROLE ON THE WALL (see page 80) to build up a picture of the children's perceptions of doctors and nurses in the relevant establishment. Other people who work there, such as receptionists, cooks, cleaners, and managers, may be added to the list of characters in similar fashion. Lists of symptoms and possible diagnoses can be drawn up. This way of working establishes a solid context within which we can add both information and new characters.

### 2. To Intervene or Not to Intervene

There is a view that children's play is sacrosanct. With this in mind teachers can sometimes be reluctant to intervene in children's pretend-corner play. A distinction should be drawn, however, between intervention and interruption. Intervention has the specific intention of helping to channel and progress the learning, whereas interruption, by definition, impedes it.

Let us explore some instances of intervention.

If the children ask the teacher to become involved in their play, this open expression of willingness to have the teacher join in clearly makes our participation easier. It might still be worth asking the student, however, to define and describe the role we should play, and it ought to be remembered that TEACHER IN ROLE (see page 74) can become intrusive even when initiated by the students if teachers are not sensitive and open to students' responses.

More problematically, however, what if children are playing apparently quite contentedly? Why should teachers intervene then? We should always bear in mind that children's play is a potent medium for learning. Acting out in play is the means by which children make sense of the world and rehearse the dialogues of life. The benefit of the pretend corner is that children take their experiences there, explore them and act them out together. In this particular classroom area teachers are able to monitor the children's perceptions and understandings about themselves, their friends, their parents, their guardians, and the world at large; but the critical question for teachers is where will that understanding lead? What will they make of the "plays" they are practicing?

Are there opportunities to reflect on what they are playing at, to analyze it and fully appreciate it? Teacher intervention in this location aims to take play out of the repetitive, stereotypical and merely experiential and transport it into the realm of appreciation and understanding.

For example, a group of children might be playing at "tea" together. While their actions and conversations might reflect some of the realities of taking tea, there will inevitably be elements of the process which are sketchy, unclear, and ill-considered. The teacher might feel it appropriate to help the children to focus on other dimensions within their dramatic play that have not occurred to them. There is, for example, much classroom evidence to suggest that girls and boys use pretend corners quite differently. In instances where girls make the tea and the boys drink it, perhaps this aspect of tea-time arrangements requires challenging.

There are other implication to what seems, on the surface, to be a relatively simple activity. After asking if it was all right to come to "tea," the teacher might join her students and "spill" the tea or "burn" herself on the kettle.

This intervention now gives the children another specific and important problem to relate to and solve. The teacher can go into and out of role (see TEACHER IN ROLE, page 74) to help them clarify and reflect on the situation. They may decide on what resources are required, where they can be found, what language and tone is appropriate to the situation, whether extra help is needed and, if so, how it can be summoned. In short, what are the implications of the event that has taken place?

In the above instance, the students were asked if they objected to their teacher's participation, and this was probably a reasonable way of becoming

"I'VE COME FOR MY MONEY. HURRY UP IN THERE! COME ON, MISSUS, I KNOWN YOU'RE IN THERE. I CLEANED YOUR WINDOWS YESTERDAY AND I WANT PAYING!"

involved, as they were *in situ* at the time, and "crashing" a tea party would probably be intrusive. There are times, however, when it may not be necessary to consult the children before intervening. If the teacher intervenes without notice from outside their immediate physical space the children are given more room metaphorically as well as physically to respond to her. For example, they might be having their tea as above when their teacher knocks at the "door." The "door" may not be answered immediately because of the surprise nature of the visit, and so their teacher may take advantage of the opportunity afforded by the delay to establish character motive and story— for example, as in the cartoon above.

This relatively straightforward approach could easily lead to an exploration of the management of budgets and financial priorities within a household.

An opening like, "Good morning, madam/sir, I've come to read your gas meter," could allow the teacher to focus on the need for vigilance when people come to their doors. Drama gives us the opportunity of considering these issues in security. If the children decide that this person whom they do not

A STUDENT WORKS ON DRAWING AND WRITING "IN ROLE."

know (within their drama) should come into their house without proof of identity, Drama creates a forum for discussion about what has happened and a means of reflecting on it and, if necessary, of retracing time and changing the course and nature of events. There may well be a place for parental involvement in such activities, as they are clearly matters of interest and importance to them. This would obviously involve careful briefing about the objectives and framework of the drama beforehand (see Parent-School Partnerships, page 129).

### 3. Writing and Reading: Integration Through Role

Speaking and Listening have been the principle components of the dramas that we have outlined thus far, but within the pretend corner it is important to integrate other activities as well. The setting up of a cafe, post office, laboratory, travel agency, or bank provides a useful context for cross-curricular work. "Customers" and "employees" can write and read in role to consolidate and advance the drama.

Menus, brochures, letters, checkbooks, advertisements, tickets, statements, and bills (see Drama and Math, below) can be designed and utilized to suit the requirements of the dramatic narrative. Real decisions can be made about budgets, cash flow and allowances, and the consequences of debt, credits, and even embezzlement may be exposed and dealt with. It is important to manage the integration of these elements in a gradual and controlled way, building up commitment and monitoring student responses as they proceed. The potential for learning in this way is virtually without limit.

## DRAMA AND MATH

This project developed out of a teacher's desire to enliven Math lessons with Year Six students. Several of the children involved were habitual truants and their Math results were poor prior to the year's start.

The teacher was particularly keen to help the children appreciate the use and value of money by encouraging them to find their own ways of carrying out mathematical tasks in a cooperative and positive environment. She decided to set up a bank within the classroom to create a context for and to satisfy these objectives. All the children were given "money" to open current accounts, but almost immediately they felt a need to spend some of their newly acquired windfalls and, accordingly, the roleplay required the establishment of shops. The students took the parts of customers and shopkeepers and within this burgeoning economy learning took place across a wide range of Math activities as well as in English, Science and Craft, Design, and Technology.

The children chose their favorite type of shop first, and a candy store was duly opened, stocked, and staffed. In time, this was followed by a sandwich shop, a drug store, a grocery store, a catalogue store, a housewares shop, and a soda fountain. Children took turns staffing and buying from the shops. "Cash" was issued daily to make up opening balances, which were deducted at the end of the day before profits were deposited in the bank.

By now the bank and the shops were generating a substantial volume of work, so much so that the bank was only open for business three days a week to allow the teacher to keep abreast of the market's growth. What was becoming especially significant, however, was that the class were so motivated by the Drama activity that they demanded the bank be open more often so that they could carry on their businesses!

The learning within the project was continually being refined and developed. The sandwich shop started to negotiate catering contracts with local shops and offered customers facilities for weddings, dances, and other functions. The drug store provided a focus for work on the capacities of medicine bottles. In the grocery store students measured the ingredients for cakes, baked the mixture, and worked out costs. The catalogue shop charged 10 percent on all sales and thereby afforded a forum for work on percentages. In the carpet and materials shop, students worked out areas and lengths and gave estimates for the decoration of the principal's office, their classroom, and the staff room. Meanwhile, at the soda fountain, the shopkeepers worked out the amounts of lemonade that would be required for birthday parties and other celebrations.

By now the classroom was humming with commercial activity, but new needs were constantly arising and plans had to be set in train to meet them. In some shops, service was deemed to be unsatisfactory, so the opening of shops was staggered to allow for staff training. Advertising and marketing budgets had to be drawn up in order to research consumer demand and attract customers. All the shops were now, as a matter of routine, considering ordering and stock control procedures. Food shops had to allow for healthy eating campaigns, and the drug store responded to animal welfare protesters who would not buy the products they were selling because they had been tested on animals.

How then was the accounting of this activity handled? Severe cash flow problems after the first week of opening the bank led to the issuing of checkbooks to all businesses. All the children made a record in their books of the daily debits and credit and the shops and bank kept similar records. Students designed their own spreadsheets (Information Technology/Craft, Design, Technology) for shops and for individual bank statements as need dictated.

It was decided to pay a regular wage to each child. Bonuses could be earned for positive attitudes and general good behavior and forfeited for antisocial behavior. This led quite naturally to free collective bargaining. The potential now existed for other banks to be set up in competition and for unions to be established to represent their members' interests. When it was discovered that someone had "cooked the books," the "offender" was traced and admitted guilt within the dramatic play. We spent some time talking about how this was often a very real problem in matters of finance. As they were discussing the situation, the students felt that they would like to explore what might occur in real life. So a mock trial for embezzlement was held. Judges, barristers, clerks, and witnesses were chosen, the paraphernalia decided upon and the proceedings set in train. This afforded the class an opportunity to learn about court procedure, consider evidence, deliberate on the facts of the case, and decide on an appropriate fate for the "offender."

All the staff, including the principal, were issued checkbooks so that they would be able to pay for the work triggered by "activity cards" written to suit individual children's and group's needs.

Examples:

You and your friends have decided to go on a camping trip. You have $250.00 each. Cost and purchase the equipment necessary for the trip.

It is your parents' twenty-fifth wedding anniversary. Organize the party, bake the cake, sort out the menu, decide on the catering arrangements and invite the guests.

The school dining room needs redecorating. You have $3000.00. Give estimates for new tables, uniforms for the cafeteria workers, plates, cups, and trays. What can the school committee afford to change?

You are unwell, and the doctor has written a prescription for three bottles of medicine (each one is 150 ml.). You will be taking a 3 ml. spoonful three times a day. How long will the medicine last?

As the project grew, the students discovered that their accounts were beginning to accumulate sizable funds. They began to make demands of the bank for more favorable rates of interest. The bank, in order to keep its customers satisfied, initiated extra interest accounts. These paid regular interest, so children became more and more familiar with percentages. Audits were also carried out on class accounts.

Tasks broadened. Holidays at home and abroad were planned, and equipment, clothing, and supplies bought for them when appropriate. For foreign trips, exchange rates were calculated and distances and gas consumption for fly/drive vacations worked out and included in budgets.

Thus, then, out of a relatively low-key beginning a whole wealth of cross-curricular areas, issues, and themes had been covered in a way that was engaging and exciting for the students. Needless to say, their math grades improved out of all recognition, and what is more, their attendance records were as good as any other class in school.*

## DRAMA AND SCIENCE

There are some subjects that lend themselves more readily to dramatic exploration than others. Science is not generally considered one of them. The following example, however, outlines what can happen within an integrated Science and Drama project.

### Flight

The Science theme to be tackled with two classes of ten-year-olds was flight. The aim of the sessions was to trace the history of flight from the earliest times to the present and to explore the moral and social issues involved. We planned an outline and focus for four forty-five-minute sessions with the teachers. They agreed to do follow-up work with the children between the sessions.

### The Drama

The classes were brought into the school hall where they discovered a man (a teacher in role) dressed in a short Greek tunic and sandals. He was oblivious to their presence as he stood at a board making sketches and calculations. The sketches were the design for a glider. Eventually, he turned round, greeted them, and explained that he was Daedalus, a Greek inventor. He recounted to them the tale of his imprisonment in a high tower by a king who wanted him to divulge his inventions. He refused, and subsequently devised a means of escape for himself and his son, Icarus. He constructed wings out of wax and birds' feathers, and they both took off. Daedalus had warned his son not to fly too close to the sun, but the boy ignored his advice. The wax holding the wings together melted, the wings fell apart, and Icarus tumbled to his death on the rocks below.

The death of his son was now spurring him on to redouble his efforts to defeat gravity. The children were keen to help and offered ideas. Their suggestions, however, ranged from jet and propeller engines to rockets and parachutes. A bewildered Daedalus begged them to pause and explain exactly what they were talking about and why they were wearing such strange

*With thanks to Becky Joyce, Headteacher, Barlows JMI.

clothing. He learned from their conversation that they were from the future. They agreed to bridge the gaps in the history of flight from his time to theirs.

In the intervening week, the children researched the topic and at the next session brought in some sketches and drawings of flying machines to show Daedalus. They ranged from Leonardo's early helicopter designs to spaceships. As the sessions progressed, students traced and explained historic developments for Daedalus.

## Issues

In order to add some tension to the drama, the class teachers decided to initiate a debate about the implications of science. One took the role of Daedalus' wife, and the other his mother-in-law. They were still mourning the death of Icarus and blamed Daedalus for his experimentation. The resulting argument revealed that advancement can come at a high price, but a popular vote established that Daedalus should continue. It is worth noting that the views expressed by Daedalus' wife and mother-in-law could easily have been represented by Daedalus himself, who, shattered by the death of his son, might well have opposed further progress, while his wife and/or mother-in-law could have urged him to carry on regardless.

Explanations of their designs were given by students in a variety of ways. They employed models and their own bodies to demonstrate their aeronautical capacity. The concept of gravity was also discussed and demonstrated to Daedalus.

The following lesson, Daedalus was in a state of great excitement. He had made a model of a hot air balloon based on details that the students had given him, and somehow the king of Phrygia had found out and offered him large sums of money to make a full-sized airplane for him. What should he do? The children wanted to know the king's intentions. The royal palace of Phrygia was set up with throne, servants, and all the trappings of wealth and power, and a scene between Daedalus and the king was acted out. It emerged that the monarch wanted the machine so it could fly over the territory of his rival, the king of the Medes, spy on his people, and drop javelins and boulders on them. Daedalus asked for leave to decide, and with the students worked out possible consequences. They felt that acceding to the king's wishes would lead to an escalation in warfare, as the king's enemy would also eventually acquire a balloon for himself, and an arms race would inevitably result. They suggested he tell the king that he would make the balloon, as long as he undertook to use it only for peaceful purposes. We set up the palace again, the king duly promised, the balloon was built, and the promise was ignored. When the children confronted Daedalus with the effects of his invention he expressed surprise at their concern for such people who were, after all, mere peasants. He told them that enemies who were captured in war were likely to be enslaved whatever their status. After the initial shock of his unfeeling response, they set up a Mede village to show him the effects of his projectiles landing on the inhabitants. We saw the mutilation, deaths, and grieving of the villagers. Immediately the reality of war became evident to Daedalus. He decided to live among the Medes and pursue his science in peace. The final scene saw Daedalus in his workshop constructing an aircraft. Outside, a delegation of Median elders were about to knock on his door. They had a request for him. . . .

As we moved through scientific history, the social and political reality of progress had been exposed by the students. The ways in which the advances of science and the implications of progress informed one another had added a significant dimension to the drama.

## DRAMA AND HISTORY
### Setting the Context

Two classes of six- and seven-year-olds, their teachers, and an advisory teacher were involved in this project. They met beforehand to discuss possible starting points for looking at History through Drama. As it was close to November Fifth, the Gunpowder Plot was mooted as a possible topic, but it was difficult to find a way in. Bonfire Night is one thing, but some sort of understanding of the background to, and nature of, injustice, religious persecution, and the social and political hierarchies and structures that characterized the Plot's reality seemed quite another for six- and seven-year-olds to grasp. However, there was agreement that the key question was how a context could be created to make some of these issues comprehensible to very young children. What might they already know that would afford a way in?

An approach was decided on that would (a) appeal to them, (b) allow the teachers to assess what their experience and understanding were, and (c) prepare the ground for a deeper exploration of the historical, political, and social factors involved in any event in History, including The Gunpowder Plot. The aim was to go beyond Guy Fawkes and his associates to consider the nature and character of power, against which the Plot was hatched. The plan was to team-teach all sixty children in the hall over a two-hour session with a fifteen-minute break at the halfway point on consecutive weeks. This was felt to be perhaps a little overambitious for the age group, but the teachers decided beforehand not to plow on with their plans if the children were at all unresponsive.

## Session One Begins: Kings and Queens

The students, we surmised, should have some knowledge about kings and queens from stories and nursery rhymes, as well as some view(s) of the current monarchy. I obviously wanted to use a dramatic approach, but it had to be low key initially if the teachers were to embrace the dramatic conventions for their own classroom practice. I thought a simple crown would concentrate the students' minds and had the potential to take on some symbolic value as the drama developed, and so we started with a "coronation."

"When I stand here in front of you, I am Mr. Ball. But if I were to put on this crown, who would I be?"

"A queen," piped one. Anxious not to knock him back, I replied, "Do you think so?" Another chimed in, "No. A king. Gentlemen are kings. Ladies are queens."

"What if I were to put it on this young woman here?"

"A princess."

"And this young man?"

"A prince."

"So now we've got a royal family."

## Now and Then

"Could we look at what the Queen does now?" I asked them to talk to their partners and tell them what they thought, and I explained that we would put their ideas on the board in a few minutes. I put an outline gingerbread figure on the board and drew/wrote their suggestions of what the Queen does: "She talks to the government at Parliament," I wrote, with a picture of the location (signified by Big Ben) next to this sentence. The list included, among other things, laying poppies at the Cenotaph and being nice to people. As we wanted to explore their perceptions of the Queen's status and role, I focused for a while on the opening of Parliament. I asked them what the Queen wears. They told me she doesn't wear a crown for the wreath-laying, but does for her Parliamentary role. We looked closer at the ceremonial.

"What does she say, then, when she goes into Parliament?"

"Hello!"

I tried it after saying that I would stand in for the Queen in her absence and enlisting them as willing members of the government.

"You mean like this? 'Hello.' "

"Hello" produced an amused "Hello" in response.

They added that she should say, "Good morning."

"Good morning," said the Queen.

"Good morning," said the government cheerfully.

"Is that it, then?" I queried. One of them suggested that they should bow and say, "Good morning, Your Majesty."

We tried it. Then I asked about the nature of her entrance.

"Slow." "Proud." "The door would be opened for her."

"The doors," rejoined another.

"Would someone like to be the doors?"

A forest of hands. The chosen "doors" stood with suitable gravity.

"How do these doors open?" I wondered.

"Servants open them."

Two servants opened the doors ceremoniously as her majesty entered to greet the government. We had moved up a gear. It was serious business now.

"Could we go back a short time?" I asked. "How does she get to Parliament?" No response. "On her bike?" I asked. Laughter. A coach was suggested, and then as further suggestions were made details were layered on their descriptions. "Horses" were harnessed, "footmen" positioned, and "guards" walked in attendance. The children directed "the Queen" and showed "her" how to sit and wave, and became "bystanders" en route with appropriate responses as well. They were bubbling, enjoying their roles and what they were finding out. But what about their perceptions of past monarchies? Now seemed a good moment to go back in time.

So far we had, with the exception of their chat in pairs, worked as a whole group. We needed to vary the activity. In smaller groups with their own teachers and two student-teachers who were also there, they now listed all the kings and queens they knew from "olden days" and said what those monarchs used to do, as far as they could. We used the outline ROLE ON THE WALL idea again, with the teachers writing down their students' contributions. Each group chose a spokesperson, and they dictated their suggestions to me as I wrote them on the board. On the right I listed the kings and queens and, where appropriate, on the left I wrote what the monarchs did. Without repeated names and actions the full list looked like this:

| Kings and Queens | What They Do or Did |
|---|---|
| Queen Mother | Visits old people |
| Queen Victoria | If she caught people stealing, she shouted at them. She had a lot of children. |
| Old King Cole | Was happy, merry |
| Queen Elizabeth | |
| John | |
| James I | |
| Arthur | Lived in Camelot |
| King Kong | Was a gorilla |

| Kings and Queens | What They Do or Did |
|---|---|
| Good King Wenceslas | |
| Henry VIII | Had six wives |
| Richard the Lionheart | |
| Humpty Dumpty's King | |
| Alfred | Burned some cakes |
| Harold | |
| Henry VII | |
| George | Lived in a castle |

This was a valuable monitoring exercise for us and we were quite taken aback by several of the responses. For example, we questioned the student who offered Henry VII about that king and she was quite adamant that Henry VII was quite distinct from other, more famous Henrys. Moreover, with the exception of King Arthur, about whom they were unclear, they were able to call out with remarkable unanimity which of the monarchs actually lived and which were fictional. Most adults would have difficulty in deciding on Arthur's existence.

I then referred the group to our earlier routine of The Queen and we compared it with the ones they had just done.

"So, let's look at what we said about the Queen and what we said about queens and kings in olden days. You've said what the Queen does. What are the differences between then and now?" After a fifteen-minute whole-group discussion backed and reinforced by mimes to indicate what specific actions looked like, we wrote down what the students told us on a sheet, as follows:

### The Differences Between Now and the Olden Days
Kings and queens in olden days . . .
bossed and led their armies (Richard the Lionheart) . . .
could have people killed . . .
could divorce (Henry VIII) . . .
were in charge of the churches.

It had taken us just over an hour to establish a view of the status of the monarch in earlier times. The ground was prepared for further exploration.

## Manifestations of Power

With children of this age, variety of activity is crucial for successful teaching. We had talked, listened, drawn, written, and played roles in groups of different sizes, but most of the children had been sedentary for most of the time. I felt the need to involve all the students in some sort of physical activity. That is not easy with sixty children, but the hall afforded us sufficient space, and

110

what we had done so far had interested them. This engagement would, it seemed to me, provide us with a context, stimulus, and structure for everyone to be on their feet and acting.

"Fine," I said. "We've talked about and seen what these kings and queens used to do. So what did they need to do all these things?" (i.e., Let's talk about power bases!)

We had a five-minute brainstorm onto the board and wrote down a range of requirements from castles, land, and palaces, through plentiful stocks of gold, money, and provisions, to an array of humanity represented by cooks, soldiers, tailors, builders, and the multifarious people required to service royal paraphernalia and panoply.

## Setting the Scene

"Right. We've talked about it. So let's set it up. Here's what you've said queens and kings need, what shall we make first?"

"A bed," someone volunteers.

"What sort of bed?"

As students described it, we constructed a four-poster with curtains, bolsters, carved figures supporting the canopy, and soldiers bristling with spears to guard the monarch's bed. The people, their weapons, the curtains, and other royal accouterments were represented by the children.

(This reminds me of the concern that adults frequently express about their experiences of embarrassment in Drama lessons, often related as "Be a tree!" In this instance a similar observation might be made about "Be a spear!" The critical distinction, however, is that "Be a tree!" was generally practiced as a decontextualized exercise, but in this case, there is every reason to "be a spear," as we have all agreed to explore ways of depicting the interior of a monarch's castle and are using our bodies in the process.)

In another part of the castle a throne was built with a canopy over it, carved dogs as armrests, and real dogs at the ruler's feet.

Elsewhere, cooks prepared dinner, tailors mended and made clothing, guards were changed, stones laid, walls repaired, and weapons manufactured and sharpened till finally the whole "castle" within the school hall was buzzing with activity.

The scene having been set, it was time to refocus the activity. I explained that the "king" could now take the throne. It was necessary for me to take this role in order to shape and structure the drama effectively. I inspected the workings of my domain. As I toured I asked the students to explain their duties and roles so as to reinforce their work and ideas, and then I sat on a canopied throne.

"Fetch my tailors!"

The tailors lined up, holding imaginary garments for the king to try. The first proffered his handiwork. I asked him to describe it. Momentarily he was taken aback. I suggested his fellow tailors might help him. They told of a black velvet cloak, inlaid with gold and purple on the inside. The king liked the style but wanted an inch off the length. He summarily dismissed all the tailors with a curt wave.

At this juncture, the children's commitment and attention were superb but what we had done so far was essentially experiential. We needed, I felt, to reflect on what had happened just then. I stood and, now out of role, I asked those who watched our last scene how the tailors felt when they were sent away.

"Sad. Unhappy."

"Anything else?"

"Angry," suggested a girl at the back.

"Why is that?" I wanted to know.

"Because they'd worked on the clothes for hours and taken care."

Back into role. No need for explanation, they will pick up on the subtlest suggestion now. I merely sit down. The chair is the throne. "Some food!" The cooks and servants rush over, miming the carrying of platters.

"What's on this plate?" is demanded of the first in line. She needs no prompting.

"Steak, your majesty."

He takes it and hands it to one of his lapdogs, who gobbles it up greedily. Servants and spectators gasp. The servants are ordered away.

"You may go now. You, guards, servants, and others who are watching, tell me, for I am curious: What have you eaten today?" Eager hands are raised.

"Water. Porridge. Bread. Cheese." Sound answers. I point at another. "Champagne," he says. I am no historian, but I presumed this was a histori-cally inaccurate statement. We hadn't located our drama in any specific period, only in "olden days," but within a castle where the monarch had guards with spears, a four-poster bed, and a canopied throne with carved dogs, I think we can safely assume that champagne would not have been drunk by servants. However, by taking this suggestion seriously I can per-haps challenge this response without undermining the students. After all, I only met these children two hours ago. For all I know, this boy might have just spoken his first word this year.

The "King" keeps playing the game. "Oh, I see one of my staff has had champagne today. How often do you drink champagne, then?"

"Birthdays," came the answer.

"Do you have anything else on special occasions?"

"Pork at Christmas."

"So what do you have normally?"

"Bread and water—and it's not very clean!"

As with the tailors' scene, we needed to stop and think about the implications of what they were suggesting. They were used to my being in and out of role by now. Children are accustomed to changing realities when they play, and now we had established the roles and structures of our current play and learning. The formal conventions I initiated at the beginning, like the crown, were now otiose for this group. All that was required was a less strident tone of voice to indicate that I was being myself.

"So the king's dogs eat better than his servants. Is this fair, do you think?"

The consequent shout of "No!" was immediate and universal.

We had, in that brief image of dog eating king's steak, made explicit the concept of unfairness, of injustice, in embryonic form.

So we came to the end of the first session. The class teachers agreed to discuss what had happened during the session to clarify and evaluate the children's impressions and understanding of what they had recreated, and they would do some follow-up work in class before next week.

## Session Two Begins: Good and Bad Queens and Kings

In the second session we aimed to look at what constitutes a good or bad queen or king in order to investigate the nature of justice and injustice in a historical context. We also were aware that an exploration of this kind might have ramifications for identifying good and bad behavior in ourselves and in others. Any historical resources we created might hopefully afford us starting points and stimuli for this.

We start with a brief recap. They remember a lot from last time. I will build on what we did last week as we progress to the next phase. As they were very responsive to roleplay last week, I will take a less prominent role today. So I start by recruiting a "queen." She is "crowned" and takes the "throne" and I narrate her story as an introduction to the next stage of the Drama.

"Once upon a time in olden days there was a young queen. She lived in a big castle with a four-poster bed, a canopied throne, her dogs, tailors, cooks, guards, and servants of every kind. She had only just become queen, but she was very clever and she knew from her history books that some kings and queens were good and some kings and queens were bad—but she wasn't sure what she wanted to be.

"Sometimes when she was alone and deep in thought, an angel sat behind her shoulder and whispered, 'Be good'; but sometimes when she was alone a devil stood behind her other shoulder and hissed, 'Be bad.' And so she wandered and wandered through the halls and rooms and corridors of her castle and thought and thought and in the end she decided that what she wanted to be most of all was wise. So she called all her advisers [pointing to the children] together into the great hall and said to them, 'I need to know from you what a good queen or king looks like and what they do, and what bad queens or kings look like and what they do. Show me. Draw or write on these great pieces of parchment (indicating sheets of paper on the walls) and when you have finished, tell me the results of your discussion. Go now!' "

The whole group split into four smaller groups of advisers (two to consider good queens and kings, two to consider bad ones), the young "queen" left her throne temporarily to work with her classmates, and they all set about their tasks filling in outline figures. This is what the four groups decided:

Good Queen/King
   Looks:
      Nice dress
   Actions:
      Is friendly, kind, not bossy; says "Good morning" and "How are you?";
      visits family; visits Houses of Parliament, government, sick people;
      helps poor people; gives food and money to the poor; is not selfish;
      won't shout; won't be cross; never says "no" to people; buys Christmas
      presents for the servants; is happy, polite, nice to work for; won't fight
      wars; watches sport; is not angry

Bad Queen/King
   Looks:
      Long, black hair; smirking, sly mouth; has mean eyes, horrible (pointy)
      crown, black gown, gold, jewels
   Actions:
      Wants to rule the world; puts people in dungeons; chops off heads;
      treats people like dirt; takes food from people; chains them up; hangs
      people; forgets about people; puts people in the stocks; only cares about
      him/herself; beheads people; stabs; wants money, gold; kills other
      kings; steals; sets bombs; sends armies to fight wars

The "queen" resumed her throne, and as her "advisers" reported back, they demonstrated what some of these actions and behavior looked like so that she was better informed when making her final decision.

THE GOOD YOUNG QUEEN SITS ON HER THRONE.

The children mimed, acted out, or created still images of the actions they had cited. As teachers we were finding these strategies very useful in helping us to monitor and assess the children's perceptions and ideas. We were able, within the dramatic format, to be observers as well as teachers—an important element in allowing us to decide more appropriately on the nature and timing of our interventions in the children's learning. Moreover, they were giving us clear indications about how they see good and bad, not only in an imaginary historical context, but also with reference to their own experiences today. At a later stage we would need to challenge some of their assumptions, but in the meantime our young queen was duly given all this advice. During this scene there was insufficient time for me to negotiate and discuss with the children a new role for myself, and in any case it would have been a distraction, as I adopted the obsequious air of an older adviser/chamberlain figure and at relevant moments made some tentative suggestions about how she might proceed. The children latched onto this idea without a problem. It was now time for a decision. She held a vote. With two exceptions the advisers felt she should opt for a good queenship, and so I rounded off this episode by narrative: ". . . And when she heard the views of all her advisers the queen decided that she would be a good queen."

It was almost break time, but I was not happy to leave it at that. We needed a hook for the next scene in her story. I asked them, "Shall we see later on how easy she finds it to stick to her decision?" They were keen. Before they went out I turned to one of the dissenting advisers and asked why he had recommended that she be a bad queen. He replied firmly, "Because bad people have all the best ideas." That was a perceptive comment. I must try to use it after the break.

## Tea and Concerns

Over tea one of the teachers looked concerned, and I asked her what the problem was. She was particularly anxious that we were reinforcing stereotypes of good and bad people by accepting the children's views, especially with regard to appearances. I agreed, but told her that I intended to challenge this and other assumptions when we started up shortly. It was crucial, however, I added, that we try to start from children's experiences and understanding, and this is what I had intended with the approach I had used.

Before the children came back, I fixed four outlines to the walls and drew a sharply pointed crowd on the blackboard. When the students came in, I asked the young queen to take her throne and began the narrative again.

## Appearances and Inner Thoughts

". . . And so the good young queen, who lived in a big castle with a four-poster bed, a canopied throne, her dogs, tailors, cooks, guards, and servants of every kind, went back to her throne and smiled on all around her. (She smiles all round.)

"Meanwhile, in the kingdom next to hers lived an evil king with a smiling, sly mouth, long black hair, and a pointed crown." (I adopt the descriptions and mime the actions as I narrate the story.)

"The king was greedy, his people were starving, and they were treated badly by him. In time he planned to take over the world, but for the moment he looked at the kingdom of the young queen next door and wanted it for himself. He knew, however, that the queen was wise and when she saw him she would see straight away that he was a bad king. But he was no fool and he had heard that the young queen had surrounded herself with wise advisers. So he took off his pointed crown and carried it to the great cupboard in the royal chambers and put it on a shelf [I mime taking off the crown and putting it on the shelf/blackboard]. Then he wrapped a poor peasant's cloak around himself and entered her castle silently by a back door.

116

"When he was there he wasted no time and searched for the great sheets of parchment of the advisers in the great hall [the children's pictures], and he looked first at the sheets that showed bad queens and kings, and he saw himself in the pictures and in the words, and then he looked at the sheets that showed good queens and kings, and he stared in wonder at them, and a tiny idea floated on the breeze of his thoughts and landed in the middle of his head, and while there it grew and grew until finally it burst into his eyes and out of his mouth till he yelled a yell of joy and triumph, wrapped his cloak about him and ran out of the castle by a back door with his black peasant's cloak flapping on his back. He ran all the way back to his own castle, through the halls and corridors, up to his royal chambers, and he slammed the door shut behind him, gasping with excitement. The bad king then went to the great cupboard where he had put his pointed crown earlier [I mime all the actions as I relate them], took out a file from a wooden chest and slowly and carefully rubbed down the pointy bits."

(It is interesting to note that although the above description was detailed and dramatic, the representation of it was very low key. The cupboard was the blackboard, and the file was just a chalk eraser. Provided that the inner logic of these dramatic conventions is adhered to consistently, children (and adults) appear to have no problem in relating to, and engaging in, the Drama.)

"When the points had been flattened by the file, the King added round bits to his crown, which was now as smooth as silk [I chalk them in]. He stood admiring his handiwork for a short while; then he took the crown [from the blackboard] and slowly put it on his head. As the crown sat smooth on his royal head, the twisted smile on his sly mouth changed, and he turned and smiled a smile of warmth, and his eyes twinkled with pleasure." The collective gasp was audible as I turned to face the children.

"So it was that the bad king went to the castle of the young queen in the kingdom next door, and he was taken into her throne room, and he said to her: 'My dear young good queen'—[aside to the children] He could see now that she was good by her nice dress and smiles.—'I am the king from the kingdom next to yours. It is my wish that our two kingdoms may join together so that we can live in strength and peace forever. Will you marry me so that this may happen as soon as possible?' "

When an adult, in role, speaks to a child, in role, in this vein, children quite reasonably tend to laugh. There was scarcely a giggle from our audience of sixty at that moment. I froze and said to the watchers, "What do you think the king is really thinking as he stands there in his rounded crown, smiling at the queen? Discuss it for a few minutes with a partner."

The queen rejoined her classmates to take part in the discussion while I held the smiling, fawning position for a short time. This was to give them an image to focus on as they talked about the king's thoughts.

To sum up my role: I had started by continuing with the story, then narrated myself into the story as the king, then I had metaphorically pushed the pause button on the story in which I was a character, holding my position as king and simultaneously using a convention rather like a theatrical aside to ask the audience what they thought was going on in my character's head. After this I circulated among the students and teachers to see how they were faring. This sub-Brechtian combination of a variety of roles and forms sounds complicated in the telling, but created no confusion in the doing.

After five minutes, the queen and I resumed our positions and asked the children to come out and voice the king's innermost thoughts. There was a huge response. One of the teachers sent the children out in ones and twos, so that we were not swamped. Two or three expressed thoughts to the effect that the king was a changed man, but the vast majority talked about his killing the queen by a whole range of devices from daggers to poison, his wanting more power for himself and fooling the queen by his subterfuge. In short, they felt that he should no longer be judged by his appearance.

The queen would have to reserve her judgment for a considerable time before she could even contemplate trusting him. Accordingly, he was rejected in his advances.

When practically every child had made a contribution to the dramatic scene, we talked about how, in real life, we should be careful about judging people by appearance and tone of voice. There was, we decided, a whole range of clues offered by others' actions and behavior that we had to assess over a long period of time before we reached any decision. Most significantly, the children decided that they would not trust people just because they smiled or were polite or well dressed or conformed to our preconceptions of looking "all right." The same criteria about judging people by appearance would also apply to negative responses, e.g., a scary or ugly looking old witch who is really a good person. (See the description of the Quasimodo project on pages 144–145.)

## How Easy Is It to Be a Good Queen?

Back to the Drama. I felt we should take a closer look at this young and "good" queen and see how compatible she would find monarchy and goodness. I outlined a new tangent to the story after securing the students' agreement to explore her future situation.

"In a forest at the edge of the good queen's kingdom there lived a lame old woman and her husband, who was a woodcutter. They scraped together a poor and humble life in a small cottage with their small son, whom they had had late in life. But one day the woodcutter died and the sad woman was not able to work to keep herself and her son. So she left the boy with a neighbor and limped off on the long journey to the queen's castle, for she had heard that she was a good queen and would help them."

We split into two groups to determine what might happen when she arrived. The class teachers were in role as the poor widow and the children set up the court and decided on the format of the meeting and its outcome. Both groups' play showed the queen bestowing food and money on an over-joyed widow. As the second performance came to an end, I added this narrative and the children moved through the developing story as I described it:

"As the grateful woman left the castle a crowd of beggars [indicating the watching children] at the back door asked her where she had got the food and money from. 'The queen gave it to me,' she said. So what did the beggars do when they heard this?"

The children rose as one and rushed into the castle demanding food and money of the good but overwhelmed queen. I shouted "Freeze," settled them down, and quietly asked them what we had learned from the last episode.

"Everyone would want something." "The queen wouldn't have any money left."

"Yes," said I, "that would be a problem for her." The session was at an end so I asked the teachers and students if they would be prepared to spend some time over the next few weeks or so working out how tenable the good queen's position would be. We established that the key questions for us were:

What are the problems she would face when she chose to be good?
How could she surmount these problems and still remain a "good"
    queen?

I promised to come back and look at what they had decided on and at any other follow-up work that they had managed to do in the meantime.

## Two Weeks Later: Keeping a Secret

When I returned two weeks later there was a plethora of written work, and various roleplays had been devised. The teachers were delighted with what their students had done in the interim.

The children had, on their own initiative, worked out several scenarios for themselves, but there were two in particular that they wanted to show me. In the first, the queen held detailed consultations with a team of advisers, and while the old woman waited for the outcome she was provided with a cup of tea. Finally, the queen offered the widow money and food provided she worked for her.

The distribution of largesse of two weeks before had been replaced by a *quid pro quo*. In the second scenario, the widow was given what she wanted provided she swore an oath not to tell a soul. The scene ended with her solemn promise and departure from the castle.

I asked the children if I might add a bit to the scene. They agreed wholeheartedly, and I said, "The old widow came limping along the path toward her cottage and as she came into sight her son, who was playing among the trees, saw her and ran toward her [I started to move toward her]. 'What happened, mother? [Slight change of voice] Did the queen give you the money?"

The girl who was in the role of the widow was clearly wrestling with her conscience, wondering whether to tell me or not, and I chipped in cheerfully. "Don't worry, mum, I won't tell anyone!"

She looked me in the eye and said, "I can see by your eyes that you're not telling the truth!"

It was a magic moment. She and I and our audience had seen in that resonant instant (a) how difficult it was in spite of promises to keep a secret and (b) how to read beyond the superficial to the person's inner disposition by a set of clues relating to eyes, tone, expression, and demeanor.

"She's quite right," I said. "It isn't easy to keep a secret, is it? Both the queen and the widow know now that they could be storing up a lot more trouble for themselves if they're not very careful."

What I had just seen served to underline for me how children can move from stereotypical responses to considered perceptions through dramatic challenges. These challenges are not viewed by them as criticisms or knockbacks but as a positive way of refining, improving, and changing their plays.

In Drama, the tension and compulsion to find out what happens next in the narrative permeates the proceedings, but the creation of powerful and resonant images also allows children (and adults) space to reflect on what they have achieved, what they have learned, what they know, and what it has to do with them and their lives.

I had learned a great deal from these children in a very short time, and together we had created a compelling context and vehicle not only for history, but for many more areas of study than we had anticipated when we started on this short and fascinating exploratory road. We had laid the foundation for further historical study. There was now a context within which incidents like the Gunpowder Plot might make more sense.

"I CAN SEE BY YOUR EYES THAT YOU'RE NOT TELLING THE TRUTH!"

## DRAMA AND TEXTS: FROM STORYBOOK TO SHAKESPEARE

Some approaches have already been outlined (see pages 21 and 49). Let us consider some others in detail.

### 1. Creating a Context

Teachers who feel that a particular novel or play text is beyond the ability of their students may be offered a way forward by the following approach. The first stage is for teachers to identify the themes and issues that the text to be studied deals with—e.g., jealousy *(Othello)*, peer group pressure *(The Crucible)*—and then to devise ways of exploring the issue with students at their level. Essentially, teacher and students work on themes by creating characters and by investigating their motivations and reactions in the process. In this way, students develop their own personal responses and create their own texts. Having experienced the learning and artistic process of creating a "text," they then come to someone else's, i.e., the author to be studied. Equipped with and confident in their own responses, they are more able to speculate on, hypothesize about, and appreciate the work of another author.

### 2. The Difficult Text: Story and Selectivity

When faced with a text that students may find difficult, is there an alternative approach to it? We will use Shakespeare as a focus for this exploration, assuming that the outlined ideas are transferable to other texts.

Shakespearean plots may need simplifying for some students, particularly in elementary school.

#### Narrative

It is essential at all levels—from the elementary level of tales from Shakespeare to the intellectual rigor of degree standard textual study—that we build from the narrative framework. King Lear, arguably one of the greatest and most challenging works in the dramatic canon, has, at its core, elements of myth and fairy tale: "Once upon a time in prehistoric Britain lived an old King and his three daughters. One day . . ."

Teachers may select specific episodes from the narrative to suit their students' interests, age, and ability, but whatever their needs, the thrust of the plot provides the foundation for further study and exploration.

#### The Text

Where does the play text fit into this scheme? Many theatre directors, in approaching Shakespearean texts with actors, edit dialogue and monologue to the bare bones to aid understanding, sometimes paring it down to single words or phrases. Later, as rehearsals progress, the metaphor, simile, and poetic flights of fancy and fantasy are added, layer on layer, to build up an appreciation of how the text is constructed and how it works. This process can work for teachers as well. It allows teachers to be faithful to the text and helps them make it approachable to students from Key Stage 2 (seven- to eleven-year-olds) upward. There is a variety of workshop techniques and strategies that foster activities approaches to Shakespeare.

### Other Scenes

It may well be that, in considering a particular play, teachers feel that a context for reading the text could be created by setting up with students a scene that helps them to focus on what has happened or what is to come. For example, when *Hamlet* opens, the King has been dead for some months, but his death is the pivot around which the plot develops and revolves. It may be valuable to set up his funeral, looking at the reactions of his friends, relatives (especially his son, his wife, and his brother), and his people. A valid rehearsal strategy may thus be recognized as equally useful in preparing students for the play, raising awareness of the implications of the King's death, supporting understanding of the text and identifying the motivations of characters.

### Activities

Students of all ages might like to write in role as Cordelia and Kent, Hamlet and Ophelia, Macbeth and Lady Macbeth, and exchange letters about their situations (see one such letter, reproduced on page 124). "Courtiers" could design, draw, and print notices of Kent's banishment from Lear's kingdom. "Mapmakers" and "architects" may draw maps of realms and plans of castles to be attacked. A whole range of similar activities will serve to reinforce the plot and add to the engagement of the students.

Some ideas will work better than others. Some are clearly inappropriate for particular age and ability groupings, but essentially it is important to bear in mind that there are alternatives to merely reading the text aloud.

### 3. Analysis and Exploration

The third possibility is that when a group has already read a text or is far enough through it to have an appreciation of plot and character background, teacher and students set about analyzing and exploring that text in greater detail.

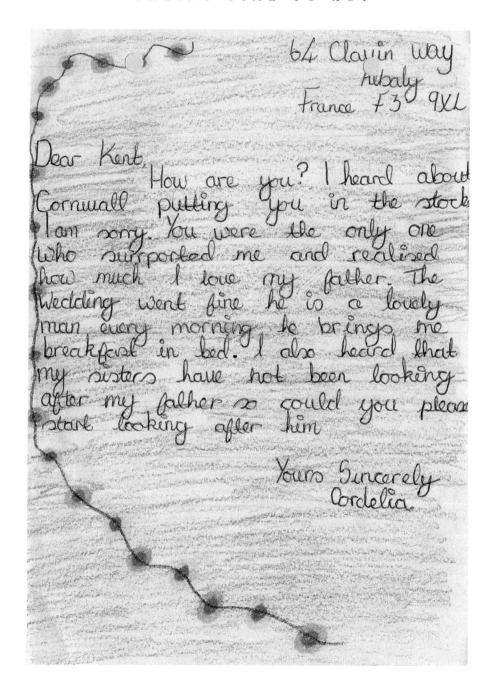

64 Clavin Way
hubaly
France F3 9XL

Dear Kent,
        How are you? I heard about
Cornwall putting you in the stock
I am sorry. You were the only one
who supported me and realised
how much I love my father. The
Wedding went fine he is a lovely
man every morning he brings me
breakfast in bed. I also heard that
my sisters have not been looking
after my father so could you please
start looking after him

                    Yours Sincerely
                    Cordelia.

Let us consider as a focus *Matilda*, by Roald Dahl. Take for example the scene where Matilda, Harry, and Mr. and Mrs. Wormwood are watching the television as they eat their meals off their knees. Some possibilities:

- Setting the scene. Work out with the group what is in the room where the scene is happening. What pictures or photos are on the wall (possibilities for drawing these) and who sits where. If useful, draw a plan of the room. Decide what American soap opera is on television— a real or a fictional one is equally acceptable. Some of the group might like to come up with dialogue for the program.
- Hotseat Characters. The group might question students playing particular roles in the scene about their characters. The TIME OUT technique (see page 80) may be employed to provide them with advice and support over their responses.
- Thoughts. You may (a) let the watchers say what they feel the innermost thoughts or feelings of the characters are (see THOUGHT TRACKING, page 75), and/or (b) create thoughts as at (a) but under more specific headings, e.g., aggressive/placating, abusive/caring.
- STILL IMAGES. Create STILL IMAGES (see page 75) of each character's dreams or aspirations.
- Create new scenes. The above ideas will reinforce character and plot. After trying them out, perhaps students might like to imagine other family scenes that Dahl did not write, using the techniques and ideas outlined elsewhere.

## CREATING YOUR OWN TEXTS: FROM IMPROVISATION TO PERFORMANCE

A group of ten sixteen-year-old girls engaged in a so-called nonacademic course known as the Certificate of Pre-Vocational Education wanted do a project on homelessness for an exhibition. The teacher, who had worked with us before, solicited our help. The students were not accustomed to working through drama; in fact, several were probably quite antipathetic toward it at the outset. We reassured them, however, that nobody would be pressured or put on the spot and that we would go at a pace that suited them. This seemed to allay any initial concerns that they had and they agreed to have a go. As the sessions progressed they became more involved and enthusiastic about this way of working.

Having studied some photographs of a wide variety of dwelling places from all around the world and having discussed homes and homelessness in general terms, we explained that we would like an image as a focal starting point for the drama on which we were about to embark together. At this stage none of us had any preconceptions at all of what shape the play might take; all we wanted was an image from which we could start.

After a few suggestions, one of the girls said, "I've got a friend, same age as me, who is going to have a baby. A little while ago she finally told her mum and dad on the same day that she had arranged to go to the prenatal clinic. She left the house at midday and didn't get back from the clinic until early evening. When she got home she found the front door locked and two suitcases on the doorstep."

There was silence for a moment, then the girls nodded. We had our image. The storyteller asked if she could play her friend and together we arranged her exactly as we thought she might look as she stood with her back to the door, facing the world, a suitcase in either hand.

It was agreed that what we were going to explore was *not* the real story. To reinforce the point we immediately invented a name for the character in our image and she became "Sharon." Sharon stood still and silent for a considerable time as the rest of us absorbed the impact of her situation.

"What is she thinking? Quietly voice her thoughts and feelings as she stands there. . ." They did so.

What could Sharon do? This was a Catholic school, and one of the first suggestions was to visit the priest for help. In an improvisation, both the priest and his housekeeper (identified by the group as a significant figure) were more concerned with her moral plight than anything else. To whom might she turn for practical assistance? Social services.

A vocal montage of bureaucratic assault was improvised. The critical awareness and knowledge of the system that the group demonstrated surprised us. The often maligned English soap opera proved to be the educational database behind much of this wisdom, but there was one other resource that informed their drama at this point. One of the young women was very quiet, almost isolated from the rest of the group most of the time. It was a little surprising when she volunteered to play a social worker assigned to Sharon's case. She started to speak to Sharon on her own. She spoke with authority and assurance. It was as though she were in a spotlight. She commanded attention and held the group as we had not seen her do until that moment. There was silence when the brief, improvised scene was over. Where had she learned to do that?

Quite simple, really. Nothing to do with academic distinction or secret reading under the bedcovers. Her sister was a social worker. Here was a young woman who did not appear to have much confidence in herself at all, who did not shine in normal class discussions, suddenly able to transfix a group of her contemporaries because a space and a context had been found that allowed her to reveal some really useful knowledge that she had acquired in everyday chat at home.

Eventually, Sharon found herself, on the advice of the social worker, in the offices of a voluntary agency committed to helping the homeless. All they could offer her was a room in a high-rise building occupied by other lonely and desperate people, many of them prostitutes and drug addicts. They devised a physical, vocal montage of the hell that they now had Sharon descending into and we paused. Where could we take things from here? What were we learning about homelessness other than it led to misery and despair?

"What'll it be like after she's had her baby?" someone asked. On her own, but with the rest of us advising from the edge of the circle, Sharon mimed some of the activities of caring for a newborn infant in the conditions we had set for her. "I think her mum would want to see her," said the girl who earlier, as her mum, had said she never wanted to see her again. That seemed to suggest a promising way forward, a shifting of responsibility to someone who perhaps could do something about Sharon's plight, an opening up of possibilities.

The vision of hell was recreated around a motionless Sharon looking down at her infant, and Mother started to weave her way through it. Displaying understandable distress and dismay, but neatly avoiding any blame for her daughter's plight, Mother started to arrange for Sharon's return home. What then happened astonished us all, not least the girl playing Sharon. She refused to go. In a remarkable piece of improvised dialogue she explained to her mother that for the first time she felt in control of her own life. The worst part of her experience after being thrown out of the family home had been that everyone who had tried to help had seemed to deny her the right to make up her own mind about anything. Her situation now, wretched as it was, at least left her the dignity of deciding some things for herself. She would be pleased to see her mum whenever she wanted to visit, but she was going to stay and make her own life with her son.

We ended the play there. We spent three further sessions recapturing the various episodes and honing them all down to a very short but very telling piece of theatre whose focus in the end turned out to be on a young person's need for independence and autonomy, a realization that was only achieved at a critical moment in the drama and that had not been predicted or planned for at all, even by the protagonist who revealed it. Her surprise at what she had discovered was one of the most interesting aspects of the whole project.

There were other interesting aspects as well though. This group of so-called nonacademic students analyzed what they had done in a lengthy discussion a few days after the performance. The level of their debate was remarkable. They talked with authority about styles of presentation and criteria for judging a piece of theatre as well as about the ideas and values they had unearthed in their drama. We occasionally offered them a word for something they were struggling to articulate—"symbolism," for example—but because they knew from experience what this meant for them they had little difficulty in assimilating such vocabulary and using it with confidence themselves.

Looked at from one point of view, this project was about producing a piece of theatre for an audience, but far more significantly it had been about a group of students using the collaborative art form of theatre to discover something about themselves and their society and then presenting the whole process of their discovery in a refined, economical form to an audience. For the first five sessions, one morning a week, we did not even consider an end product. We were building a play, but not one for anyone else. It was only when we had discovered what we wanted to know that we thought about saying it for others. The shift in emphasis from product to process is an important one if theatre really is to be, as Peter Brook (1988, page 15) claims, the bringing together of "a multitude of different visions." It takes time and trust, both in the process and in each other as participants, but it is worth it.

Another example of a rather simpler process of play making was a project that brought together twenty-four boys and girls age fourteen and fifteen from a suburban comprehensive school—John Lennon's old school, in fact—and twelve boys and girls age twelve to seventeen from a neighboring school for students with severe learning difficulties. We decided to base our drama on Maurice Sendak's picture storybook, *Where the Wild Things Are.* We had six weeks, a little over an hour a week, before we were due to take part in a celebration of work done by special schools throughout the city.

Again, we had little notion of what the final product might look like. Our initial concerns were to forge a completely integrated company out of two groups of young people with apparently not a lot in common, meeting for the first time, and to get this company playing and thinking together as quickly as possible. Thanks to the excellent good will and skill of all the youngsters, their teacher and care staff, and a parachute, we got there within a couple of weeks. The parachute proved a useful energizer and ice-breaker and later a turbulent ocean on the way to where the wild things are. By the fourth week we had spent some time physically recreating elements of the story—bedrooms, boats, and wild things, in full rumpus—composing atmospheric music and one lovely song, and exploring what exactly might be the nature of these wild things that Max visited—or rather, that visited Max. We questioned whether the wild things that possess a boy would be the same as those for a girl, and soon Max became Maxine, Queen of all the Wild Things, played jointly by two girls, one from each school. How might Maxine handle her different wild things—fears, desires, drives—without taming or destroying them? We had only just started to engage with this important question when the demands of the imminent show obliged us to stop and focus on shaping some of the work we had already done into a brief performance piece. With no more than a total of two hours' rehearsal ahead of us we had already decided simply to present Sendak's story through physical theatre, music, and choral narration. If we had had longer we might have incorporated some of our investigations into wildness; on this occasion we kept that part of the drama to ourselves. What the audience enjoyed was the story of Maxine, holding hands, as her bedroom furniture grew into a forest and a silken ocean came tumbling by with a boat that took her to become Queen of all the Wild Things, where she led the wild rumpus and then sent them off to bed without their supper, becoming lonely and sailing back over a year and in and out of weeks and through a day and into the night of her very own room to find supper waiting for her . . . still hot. The whole company, except the musicians, and of course Maxine, created all the moments of the story. The result was like a dance as the bodies wove together to form the shifting images, in movement and in stillness, accompanied by music and their own choral narrative.

As teachers, we may have felt that the most important learning had taken place in the first four weeks: learning about each other; learning about how to accept differences and work together without fear or embarrassment; learning about coping with the "wild things" that threaten to control us if we don't have at least some understanding of them. Whatever our priorities, however, there could be no denying the value of the simple presentation of Sendak's evocative fable as a celebration of and a joyous conclusion to that earlier work. We performed it again, two weeks later, for the students, staff, and parents of the special school and took the opportunity of analyzing the experience of the whole project with the students. They recognized what they had learned from it and what they had gained.

## DRAMA AND PARENT-SCHOOL PARTNERSHIPS

Adults are wary of Drama. As we mentioned in the Teacher's Tool Kit, disconcerting experiences in school and subsequent concerns about being made to look silly or self-conscious have tended to deter people from roleplay. Drama, however, when sensitively employed, can be a vital force in effective and exciting work with parents. What exactly can it offer for parents' groups, then? Educational Drama focuses on people's actual experience and uses it as the starting point and basis for interacting and developmental work. It addresses concerns and interests through the dialogue of dramatic form. While Drama helps people to explore issues at their own level, it can also be a means of supporting parents in passing on skills and learning to the children.

We will cite some examples of Parent School Partnership/Drama projects that have been tried and may be useful models for those who want to have a go at new initiatives and ways of working.

## 1. Devising a Play

In this instance a group of parents wanted to mount a play of their own. The first stage of the project began with a brainstorm of topics that interested them. The two key themes that emerged were neighbors and the history of the community. Stories of characters, some alive, others dead, and incidents from local life were exchanged and this formed the foundation for improvisation and narrative building.

A story line was hammered out over several sessions. Scenes were added and discarded as research unearthed new facts and angles. A successful application was made to the then Merseyside Arts Association to fund a professional writer who would watch the cast in workshop, discuss the scenes devised so far, and impose structure and shape on the narrative.

The play was then written, rehearsed, and performed by the parents at six venues in the community with considerable success.

## 2. Working in the Classroom

The foregoing procedure worked well, but the skills, strategies, and techniques learned and employed in the process were not at that time transferred to the classroom, although they clearly had classroom application; for the confidence, articulateness, awareness, expressiveness, and cooperative dynamic fostered in rehearsal, workshop, and performance stood some of the participants in good stead for classroom work later.

In this second example, however, the parents from a different school designed and planned a project specifically for classroom work. First of all, the teacher provided a theme: "Life in the 1950s." The parents prepared a scenario to involve the students. After only one session the parents, horrified at the students' sexist attitudes, decided that the theme had to be adapted to focus on gender stereotyping. Later the students took the theme in a different direction, i.e., the problem of bullying. The parents were able to deal

PARENTS DISCUSS THE DRAMA WITH PUPILS.

positively with, challenge, and discuss the fixed values and views that the boys especially were propounding.

At the outset it was crucial that the parents progressed at a pace that they felt happy with in terms of the process. Likely student responses to the piece were discussed in detail and worked on until everyone was confident with the material and the way of working. Members of the group prepared and practiced together, then team-taught with partners who assisted if the person leading a group discussion in the classroom needed support and advice. Different sizes of student groups were worked with and the parents developed open and flexible responses to the children's ideas.

After each of four hour-long sessions with the students, the group talked about what had transpired, suggested improvements, and planned the next one. A dialogue with the teacher, who was very encouraging and remarked on the positive reactions of her students, promoted two way feedback and evaluation of the work. Everybody involved felt the coming and working together of parents, teachers, and children was a profitable, revealing, and enjoyable partnership in which all had learned a great deal.

An unexpected outcome of this work was the production of a code of conduct to prevent bullying in the class, drawn up by the students with the help of the teacher (independently of the parents) to which they adhered stringently.

## 3. Assemblies and Work with Other Parents' Groups

In this example, another group of parents who had offered to present an assembly to their junior school chose (once again) the theme of bullying and, over six Drama sessions lasting an hour each, worked on devising a five-minute play to show the students. The characters were worked out, the structure of the piece formulated, likely responses of the children considered and possible lines of development planned. All the parts were played by the group members. The play was open ended and the intention was that, after the presentation, small teams of parents would work with one class each and come up with feasible endings to the dramatic narrative.

The play looked at the story of a girl who was being bullied in school. Within the presentation two possible solutions were suggested, but these were shown to be limited in their effectiveness, and so children had to come up with better strategies for dealing with the bullies in the play and consequently in real life as well. The children's suggestions were acted out by parents in front of the whole school, and the best courses of action agreed and noted by the assembly. Dealing with large numbers of children in an active forum proved a difficult but fascinating learning experience for the group, but they felt it would be useful to do more detailed work with a smaller number; so a Year Six class was chosen and two lessons were led by parents.

After each lesson the parents discussed classroom management, lesson content, and worked out ways of improving their own teaching skills. Through the experience of this project the parents came to have a sound understanding of teachers' roles and the concerns they have.

Some weeks after their work in the classroom, the parents were invited to a parents' day in another Parent-School Partnership across the city, and they made a successful and skillful contribution. This involved putting together a presentation about their work to a group of about eighty people, leading workshop sessions with groups of between fifteen and twenty-five parents, teachers, and community workers, and giving feedback on their work to a plenary. The Parent-School Partnership workers and parents themselves commented on how the group's confidence and self-esteem had flourished in this open, flexible, and cooperative approach.

## ON LOCATION

Most of the Dramas referred to so far have been based in school buildings, but there is a plethora of out of school locations where teaching also takes place. The "school trip" is often a memorable experience, but Drama can make it even more resonant and exciting.

In the regular course of their school life, students visit museums, galleries, castles, historic houses and buildings, cathedrals, canals, parks, nature reserves, archaeological sites, and more. All these places lend themselves to dramatic exploration and interpretation. Dramatic input into these events can range from a few minutes to framing the whole experience within a drama.

### Conwy Castle: The Whole Experience

Along the coast of North Wales are five of the finest thirteenth-century castles in the world: Fflint, Rhuddlan, Conwy, Caernarfon, and Beaumaris. They were all built in the late 1200s at the command of Edward I, arguably England's greatest administrator king, to protect the English corn supply on its route from Anglesey to Chester and beyond against the depredations of fierce Welsh tribes. By the 1280s, Llywelyn, a Welsh guerrilla leader who had formally been recognized as Prince of Wales by Henry III but had refused to pay homage to the new king, was dead, but Edward knew well enough that the Welsh threat was always likely to menace English interests if communications and allegiance were not adequately secured into the foreseeable future. To this end, he enlisted the services of the finest contemporary castle builder, Master James of Savoy, to fortify the Welsh coast. An ambitious castle building program was initiated. Conwy and Caernarfon Castles were completed within four years, and a state-of-the-art concentric castle was later started at Beaumaris on Anglesey but never finished, as the other two fortifications had by then rendered resistance all but negligible. These three castle are still in good order, but as generations of British schoolchildren clamber over their ramparts on school visits, how can they engage with an understanding of military strategy, tactics, design, and technology, and their thirteenth-century application against the Welsh? The problem is that more often than not tours can tend to be unfocused and random and the locations are seen as mere shells. There is little sense of the castles' original significance and intent and studying it has little real meaning for students of today.

In March 1992, a motley troupe of fifty nine-year-olds from an inner city Liverpool school marches toward the main gate of Conwy Castle. In role as fisherfolk, farmers, and craftspeople, they approach the castle's looming

KING EDWARD IS PLAYED BY A TEACHER IN ROLE. NOTE THE MINIMAL COSTUME.

towers, proudly carrying the banners of their tribes (see below, "Preparing for a Visit"). Accompanied by an apparent Welsh quisling, Morgan (teacher in role), they have come ostensibly to pay fealty to King Edward, but in reality to spy out the strategic weaknesses of his new castle. Edward is a teacher in role. He creates an imposing silhouette as he stands arms akimbo on the inner curtain wall. He is dressed in a necessary cagoule against the biting wind off the Irish Sea, and equipped with fluttering blue cloak and silver cardboard crown. As they enter the courtyard, Edward, endorsed by Morgan, warns them to attempt no subterfuge or deception as his (fictional) archers are now watching from behind the slits in the towers. The castle, he explains, looks as it does because it is under construction. On completion, it will last for a thousand years, a majestic and invincible white bulwark against their aspirations. As tourists stroll round the walls, Edward berates Morgan and includes the bemused spectators in the dramatic narrative by demanding to know why "these workers" are staring at and mocking the proceedings rather than getting on with their jobs. Their laughter subsides and the atmosphere intensifies as Edward summons the tribespeople to his presence chamber and turns on his heel. Morgan briefly talks to the students about the implications of Edward's power and the need for cunning to circumvent him.

And so the King sat awaiting the Welsh, high in his chamber. When all were assembled, he demanded gifts of allegiance from them. They duly laid gifts before him, and everything progressed without incident until the farmers' spokesperson stepped forward and proclaimed, fortissimo, "This the gift we bring you, Longshanks." With that, he delivered a neat but vehement globule of spit at the king's feet. The insult demanded a response from Edward. He called Morgan to his side, whispered in his ear and stalked out. Instead of responding directly to the child-farmer, he heightened the suspense by creating uncertainty and leaving an uneasy gap in the action. Morgan used the space to refocus on Welsh feelings and reactions, and to intensify reflection of the connotations of the king's and his army's presence in their country.

Edward returned in due course and calmly announced that they were free to wander around his castle, examine it, marvel at its design, and despair at its impregnability. As the king left, Morgan urged them to seek out every recess of the castle and note any weak points so that, when they had returned to their villages, they could plan an attack. They explored each stairway; made notes of the thickness of walls; studied the design of machicolations and the relative strength of the west and east barbicans; they estimated the width of the garderobes and weighed up the possibility (and desirability) of clambering through them into the stronghold at dead of night. In short, as potential attackers, they cased the whole joint.

After deliberation with Morgan, they decided that a full frontal assault would not work. They determined to swear an oath of allegiance to the King, lull him into a false sense of security, and plot his downfall from the mountain villages. The oath was composed and sworn by all in the King's presence. As they were about to depart the courtyard with Edward's blessing, he suddenly called them back and demanded that, as a sign of good faith, they hand over the banners that they had so carefully constructed prior to the visit (see below, "Preparing for a Visit"). The students were close to real as well as imagined revolt as the king took the banners and flung them to the ground, promising that they would be torched as soon as the students had gone. The discarded banners were now a powerful symbol that was scored into their consciousness. They now had his permission to leave.

Back in the busy Welsh street, the motley troupe looked back on the tourist attraction above them. The castle had reverberated with powerful images of realpolitik: strategy, technology, the ruthlessness of unbridled power. These resonances would endure long and remain vivid in the participants' minds.

They had looked at and seen through the castle. Now they knew.

## Before the Visit

### 1. Opening a Dialogue

Teachers may be happy to try out drama ideas on visits, but may be unaware of an institution's attitude toward work of this kind. Most places want to accommodate visitors, but it is important to contact the educational liaison person at the venue, find out what their views and principles are, and negotiate from there. In locations where there is a roleplay team of actors on site, it is well worth contacting them about their work and, if possible, see them in action to prepare the children. This will maximize the benefit from the visit (see below, "Roleplay in Residence").

It is important for teachers to be clear on their educational aims and objectives prior to any meeting, to have some idea of the kind of activities that they have in mind, and not to be overambitious. If, for example, there are valuable and breakable objects in the location, this will inform the teacher's choice of activity.

Wherever possible, teachers should visit the location beforehand.

### 2. Internal Communication

It is equally important that the above-mentioned link person consult with guides/volunteers/interpreters so that they appreciate what is going on and what is appropriate. We were once involved in a particularly gripping dramatic moment where a "trial" was being conducted in a cathedral's chapter house when suddenly a guide came in and started to expound loudly on the architecture of the room to a group of tourists. The dramatic moment was lost thanks to his interruption. There was clearly an element of crassness from the interloper, but a simple memo communicating the project to staff could have preempted the problem. Bitter experience has taught us that people who are not consulted are often obstructive. These suggestions on prior contact are simply designed to alert teachers to some of the difficulties that may occur, not to deter them from Drama practice.

## 3. Preparing for a Visit

The amount and character of the preparation will be determined by the nature of the visit itself. It can vary from a brief explanation of what will happen when students arrive at the location to a series of developmental sessions, involving roleplay and researcher. In the instance of the visit to Conwy, several different strategies were employed in the course of the preparation, and these might serve to exemplify something of the variety of preparation that can be undertaken.

### Designing a Castle: Low-Key Roleplay, Designs, and Technology

The key question that informed the preparation was: "If you were Edward I in 1284, what would you do to protect your supply route from the Welsh?"

We started the lesson by suggesting that the children take the roles of lords and ladies of Edward's court, who had fought many long, hard campaigns with him and given him excellent advice in the past. A teacher in role as Edward asked what they felt he should do next to underpin English interests. Materials were provided: a map of the coastline that showed existing castles (Fflint and Rhuddlan), towns, topographical features, and roads; and plans of the castles that already existed.

On the basis of the evidence, a unanimous decision was taken that castles should be built. The students were then given the task of choosing the best locations for the castle and of coming up with a design that best met their needs.

They decided, without any awareness at this stage of the historical accuracy and contemporary actuality, that a castle should be built at Deganwy (across the river from the actual location at Conwy), but simultaneously recommended that another castle should be built further along the coast to safeguard against attack from the rear, and a third should be built on the island of Anglesey just for good measure. This was remarkably close to the decision that Edward himself made. Each design group took turns to present its own drawings and plans, and the audience gave positive and supportive feedback. "Edward" thanked them for their pains and said the outline plans would be forwarded to Master James for his perusal. Later the whole group looked at Master James' actual designs and they compared and contrasted what had influenced his and their plans.

### Looking at Tactics: Thinking About the Location's Environment

In order to emphasize the importance of the castle building program, we looked at the topography of the region and (this time in role as Welsh tribespeople) worked out the best ways of attacking the English. We worked on a number of set pieces, analyzed them, and discussed their appropriateness. There then followed a sophisticated discussion of the pros and cons of guerrilla tactics and the various considerations that inform military strategy. The depth and quality of this work and student attentiveness was well beyond expectations and, most importantly, gave them a disposition toward the site that would make the visit all the more focused and meaningful.

### The Local Population: Building a Commitment to the Activity

The preparation on the character of the local people during the thirteenth century was easily planned and extremely useful. This particular area of focus is often a productive one to explore prior to a visit. Many of the locations are likely to be historical and the aspirations, character, and occupations of the contemporary population are crucial to a fuller understanding of the place. We talked at some length about food, subsistence, housing, clothing, jobs, about social intercourse within their families and the wider community, their feelings about the land, the English, nature, and the gods whom they worshipped. They made banners and chose emblems of their tribal occupations and carried them ceremoniously and with pride.

And so when they finally approached the lowering towers of Conwy they had a commitment to and belief in their roles that would not be diverted by the presence of other visitors nor the occasional blare of distant automobile horns.

### On The Way: A Few Minutes . . .

If teachers in the early stages of Drama practices are not totally confident or convinced about trying things out *in situ*, there may well be an opportunity to try some Drama on the way to the venue. For example, a visit to a museum gallery where there is a display about the Western Front could be enhanced by teaching the students songs from World War I to sing on the way. Out of this might develop an awareness of the feelings of soldiers as they traveled toward the front.

After the pleasantries of song, a period of quiet reflection on arrival at the museum would allow them the opportunity to speculate on what soldiers' expectations of the conflict might be.

Teachers could choose to line their students up outside the bus in military order and march them toward the museum humming "It's a Long Way to Tipperary" and other songs of the period, quietly and more slowly now, in contrast to their previous enthusiasm.

A journey to any venue can be seen in any number of different narrative contexts. Teachers can design simple maps with appropriate landmarks that the children must read to check that they are going the right way to the castle they are spying on, or the park where the treasure is buried, or the house where a rebel leader is hiding. Besides being exciting and of obvious educational value, this sort of activity has the advantage of keeping students gainfully employed and also of getting them in the frame of mind for their visit.

## In the Locations: Revamping Worksheets

The format that some worksheets employ has little else to recommend it except the testing of observational skills. This procedure has the disadvantage of encouraging children to look for closed answers to immediate questions rather than to learn about the wider aspects of a location's use, architecture, history, and topography. Sometimes questions form part of a trail where, as in orienteering, children discover a symbol, sign, or letter at specific points on their maps.

Drama, however, can give this activity a far more powerful impetus. This is achieved by investing the acquisition of answers with more tension and compulsion. It sets them in a narrative context where the children have to find solutions as a matter of urgency—or even before it is too late. . . .

### Maps and Clues

On one visit students in role as Native Americans have arrived at a local park to consult the Great Spirit of the Ancestors; for the signs have told them some evil will soon befall them.

They are given maps to read. At each location is a letter or symbol. This allows for differentiation among the groups and focuses on means of communicating. The choice of symbols and their placement also encourages reflection on the environment and humankind's relationship to it. When all the clues have been found and pieced together they give details of what to do next. Different groups have different maps so that the search is not competitive, but each group's findings are an integral constituent of the whole message. The narrative thrust of such an exercise injects the activity with urgency, relevance, and meaning.

In another instance, set in the Cathedral of Notre Dame (as played by the Anglican Cathedral in Liverpool), the children, in role as French people of the fourteenth century, are hailed by a darkly crouching figure in the gallery 150 feet above them.

He calls to them to come and find him and throws maps into the void. As they slowly flutter to the great stone floor, the children grab them eagerly. They inspect Quasimodo's freehand drawing for clues to his whereabouts. Their explorations take in the unseen structures of the vast cathedral's belfry, chambers and hidden recesses. They interpret clues, events, and incidents as they proceed on their quest.

### Computer Printouts

In a Victorian country house, a group of time travelers arrive in the past to identify the cause of an accident in 1888 where a child died while skating on thin ice.

In several locations they will witness events enacted, hear sounds, or find pieces of evidence. Like detectives, they have to make sense of the various clues and reconstruct the past. They must identify a person they have encountered (not the victim) and somehow persuade him/her not to act in a particular way, so that they can stop the accident from happening. It is crucial that the child who died lives, because she is the potential discoverer of a scientific advance that will save the world from imminent destruction. The problem is that they have only forty minutes before they return to their own time. The computer prints out their instructions as the clock ticks down. . . .

This activity looked at a wide range of curricular areas and involved actors, Information Technology, Music and Media, but it serves to illustrate the effectiveness of worksheets that utilize this approach. The conceit of changing history is a familiar one and accessible to children from story lines like that of *Terminator*. Drama builds on images and conventions with which students are familiar and to which therefore they can react all the more readily.

## Roleplay

The intensity, frequency, and length of a roleplay are entirely at the teacher's discretion. The suitability of the space and the attitude of the keepers have to be taken into account. Roleplay can be a potent addition to any teacher's armory, however, even with minimal intervention.

### Displays, Artifacts, and Artwork

In front of a display of an Egyptian pyramid, the children are asked to look at the design before them and, as architects and designers, to recommend additions to the construction to circumvent grave robbers. Within this activity they are also asked to put themselves in the shoes of robbers in order to do their job effectively. It adds to the tension when the teacher, as pharaoh's priest adds, as an afterthought, that death will, of course, be consequent upon failure. This strategy does not require costume, accent, or effect, only the display on which the group is focusing.

In another part of the gallery, a class surrounds a totem pole and the teacher asks for silence as she addresses the class:

> "People of the tribe, as your elder, I have to tell you the harvest has failed us once again, but there is yet hope for us. A man has come in a dark suit from the city. He wants to give us money for our giant totem and he will take it with care and respect on his long, many-wheeled wagon to his big museum far away. Soon they will arrive. What do you think we should do?"

The religious and social significance of the totem for the tribe and the consequences of its removal are revealed in the dramatic discussion that ensues.

In an art gallery, a class looks at a picture of a woman staring intently toward the observer. The children, in role as art historians, have been told that this picture is one of a pair but the other painting has been lost. It is explained that the original intention of the artist was that the two works should face each other across the room in which they were to be displayed. The students' task is to work out and construct the sight that the woman in the picture might be looking at. This is essentially the creation of a physical, emotional, and analytic response to a work by the impetus of Drama. Although it is not a true account of the painting's provenance and artist's intention it is, in our view, perfectly acceptable to construct this kind of fiction provided that this is, at some stage, made clear to the students. Drama in Education is essentially about saying "What if . . . ?"

### Roleplay in Residence

Where museums, galleries, or sites offer dramatic experiences as part of their educational and visitor service, it may be possible to negotiate a slightly different format to accommodate teachers' specific needs or even, where the teacher has more experience of Drama, suggest more significant changes. The following two examples are at opposite ends of the spectrum of adaptation.

## 1. Low Key: Planetarium

In the course of a Drama project about space, a group of Special Needs students had met an "alien" from a distant galaxy, whom they christened Thurl. This being had grabbed their attention, and they were desperate to find ways of communicating with it and learning about its planet—wherever it might be. A trip to the local planetarium seemed an appealing bridge into further research. The planetarium program with its sound and lighting effects was exciting in itself, but the question and answer session that followed it would be less likely to hold their attention. Some emendations were suggested to the staff.

Instead of the curator answering questions as himself, we asked him to respond as an android. He was thrilled with the idea and rigged up a mike which was fixed into the public address system with reverberation turned up high. Thurl accompanied the students to the show and as it began, pointed up into the darkness of space. At the end, Thurl simply stood there in the middle—a focus for their investigations. The first question came: "How does Thurl get to work in the morning?"

"By bike," the android intoned, "But sometimes he commutes by rocket car or moving walkway."

This humorous reply immediately tapped into the children's experience but it also engaged them with elements of science fact, like a children's story rendered three-dimensionally. We had merely requested a monotone, but it was ending up a full-blown performance with accompanying effects. The other elements were not necessary, but they were certainly enhancing the experience and, as sometimes escapes our consideration in a Drama, the roleplayer himself was deriving pleasure and learning from the experience. And why not—provided he was not distracting the students?

To the question "What planet does Thurl come from?" the android replied by citing the characteristics of various planets and the likelihood of their being able to sustain a living being like Thurl. As the curator continued to respond, it was remarkable how, almost paradoxically, the monotone of his voice made some of his driest answers interesting rather than boring, as the students listened intently to android speech patterns and scanned his eyes for the slightest flicker of emotion.

By the end of the session, they had assimilated copious facts about the solar system that might have scarcely made an impression within a more conventional setting.

## 2. High-Key: Emigration Galley

This example is set in the reconstructed hold of a nineteenth-century emigrant ship. Here, schoolchildren and other visitors are asked to assume the roles of emigrants and are offered the experience of encountering various characters on their voyage to America. A teacher who was planning a visit to the ship was concerned that there would be little opportunity during the experience to reflect on what was happening. The suggestion was made that the children should have two roles—those of emigrants and those of historians, studying emigration from a modern perspective. A page from a diary, supposedly written by a passenger on a ship bound for America in 1843, was presented to the class. The extract, however, was ripped and illegible in places. The children would time travel back to 1843 to discover what the missing bits might have contained. In order not to alert the people of the nineteenth century to the deception, the class would have to disguise themselves as emigrants of the period. The teacher, as "time guardian," had a wand of light (à la Star Wars light saber), and when this was illuminated by the teacher, time stopped, the actors froze, and questions could be asked of the children, such as:

> What do you think she is thinking at this moment?
> What do you think the sickness is that she is referring to?
> What are the implications for us as passengers and historians?
> What questions would you like to ask her?

The advantage of this approach is that the children can be both involved in and stand outside the proceedings. The museum was delighted to accommodate this approach and adopted it themselves on future teachers' courses.

With the roleplay format that was already in use in the museum, it would have been quite possible for the teacher and class to think about the experience back in school or even to recreate elements of the experience for themselves as a focus for discussion. They could still do this, but within this model they also had the opportunity to reflect at the very moment of impact.

## BIG LOCATIONS: AN INTRODUCTION

Rooms, buildings, and environments can make superb locations for dramas. When planning a drama in such a location, however, it is crucial to take its qualities into consideration. Where possible, they should not merely be used as two-dimensional stage sets but as three-dimensional, living areas into which the participants have entered. In a very real sense, they are there. The ambiance of the great hall of a country house with its oak panels and armorial artifacts, the acoustics of a cathedral's vast belfry, the confined space of a spiral staircase lit only by candles, a lone teepee set in the middle of a field, a castle's tower with a torn flag fluttering fitfully atop it are dramatic in themselves, but they also confirm and underline students' engagement and belief in what they do. In such instances the setting assumes a dynamic being treated almost as a character in its own right. Refer to the location with the participants, talk about its special qualities. Move around the place, where possible, reflect on what it represents, allow it to resonate within the activity. Consider involving its light, its dark, its space in the drama. If the place is not fully integrated into the activity from the outset, its ambiance may even distract from the activity itself. The illustration that follows outlines ways in which these suggestions may be interpreted.

## Quasimodo: Working Across the Curriculum

The project under consideration was to take place at the Anglican Cathedral, Liverpool, one of the world's largest. The project's aim was to use Victor Hugo's Notre Dame de Paris as a vehicle for teaching History, Geography, English, Personal and Social Education, and Equal Opportunities through the art form of Theatre.

## Preparation: Visiting the Location

A preliminary visit with the Cathedral's helpful Education officer immediately established the dramatic potential that the location offered: the vast, cavernous central space with its 150-foot inner tower and gallery and the wonderful acoustics of the circular chapter house had obvious possibilities. However, behind the highest Gothic arch in the world lay a host of other superb locations: spiral staircases that led tortuously to a long triforium gallery and upward into the remote dark viscera of the building. High in the tower, 200 feet above the ground, was a set of three dark chambers: the lowest, a bellringers' chamber with cast iron beams supporting a concrete roof; the second, a low room where the sounds of the largest rings of bells in the world were dampened to protect human ears; and finally, the belfry itself, where even the smallest bell would deafen any interloper. Inside the belfry itself the louver windows were so vast that the space created its own atmospheric conditions—its own unique atmosphere.

## Planning

In order to take full dramatic advantage we had to work with the location and not against it. Each of the locations had a characteristic ambiance that had to be intrinsic to the plot. The scenes were planned and rehearsed by actors who played Quasimodo, the Archdeacon Dom Claud Frollo, Captain Phoebus, and Esmeralda. Employing professional actors involved funding, and the Regional Arts Board gave a grant toward fees. In other Drama projects actors have been recruited from senior secondary schools, and they have performed and facilitated work for younger children from neighboring primary schools. This has been a useful means of fostering creative, educational liaison between elementary and secondary schools.

In the course of the planning, a number of issues arose.

## 1. The Children's Role in the Proceedings

What role should children take in the drama? As the events were acted out, would they be able to influence or change them?

It was felt appropriate that the children should roleplay fifteenth-century citizens of France visiting the great cathedral of Notre Dame, whose construction they had helped to fund. To this end, they would spend an hour in the crypt of the cathedral prior to the performance, thinking about the period, investigating contemporary attitudes, and getting into role. Pictures, time lines, photos of Notre Dame itself, and research material detailing dress and occupations would be used in the preparation.

It was decided that when the drama was underway, the students could not reasonably affect the action, as there was not the logistical flexibility to act out divergent story lines. However, it was felt to be crucial that there should be space to reflect on and, within limits, to make decisions and judgments about the action. The chapter house would be the area to which we retired during the course of the day to think about the action, to deliberate about characters, to try to judge Quasimodo, and to suggest additions or refinements to the narrative.

## 2. The Teacher's Role

Another concern was the need for a guide, mentor, and facilitator as students promenaded around the cathedral. The proposed solution was for a teacher to take the role of Frollo's younger but estranged brother, the student Jehan. He would be both in the action and out of it. He, like the children, would be coming to visit the cathedral, but would constantly ask them what they thought, why this or that was happening, and who was responsible for the unfolding events.

## 3. Enhancing the Atmosphere

The conventional tourist ascended the tower by lift. We were allowed to use the spiral staircase. The cathedral agreed to supply long, thick, altar candles to light our way. The flickering, eerie shadows and the smell of smoke reinforced the sense of period and mystery.

Another feature of the cathedral was the magnificent organ. A theme tune was written to accompany a scene where the gypsy Esmeralda was led across the central space to her execution. As the procession of actors and children reached the midpoint, Quasimodo emerged from the shadows and carried her off to sanctuary. The slow and quiet theme was transformed into such a powerful fortissimo that the stone floor shook. The same motif was introduced at the beginning of the drama by Esmeralda when she played it on her recorder. Quasimodo would suddenly appear in the gallery 150 feet above her and sing words to her accompaniment, immediately establishing an uncanny rapport between the two characters.

## 4. Reaching the Unreachable: Multi-media Possibilities

A limit of forty children was imposed at each performance. This was necessary, as any larger number than this would have made it difficult for all to see. Safety was paramount, and although we were going high up inside the cathedral, we were not intending to visit any exposed or dangerous places. We planned to make up for this lack by filming a five-minute chase sequence in dangerous locations. The result was spectacular. After the "sanctuary" scene, we told the children of a giant oracular statue in the crypt. When people stared into its eyes (two television screens set within a huge papier-mâché head), they could see events unfolding elsewhere. At the appropriate moments, participants would see Esmeralda and Quasimodo being chased through dark tunnels and passages by Frollo, out along high balconies; and finally, when Frollo appeared to have them cornered on the outside roof of the cathedral, Quasimodo rappelled off the tower with Esmeralda clinging precariously to his back.

The filming took place over two days with a grant from the cathedral's education budget. Two television cameramen and a feature film director, Chris Bernard Letter to Brezhnev), worked from our storyboards, and a local television company gave us free access to on- and off-line editing facilities.

## 5. Areas of Learning

We had several learning objectives planned from the drama. History would be a key element and so, too, English communication skills. But Geography could also be brought into play. The activity would be integrated into the dramatic narrative. At the outset Frollo would ask the students to convey an important message to his bellringer, Quasimodo. As Frollo left, Quasimodo would appear seconds later in the tower high above them. The children's

QUASIMODO SURVEYS THE PANORAMA BELOW.

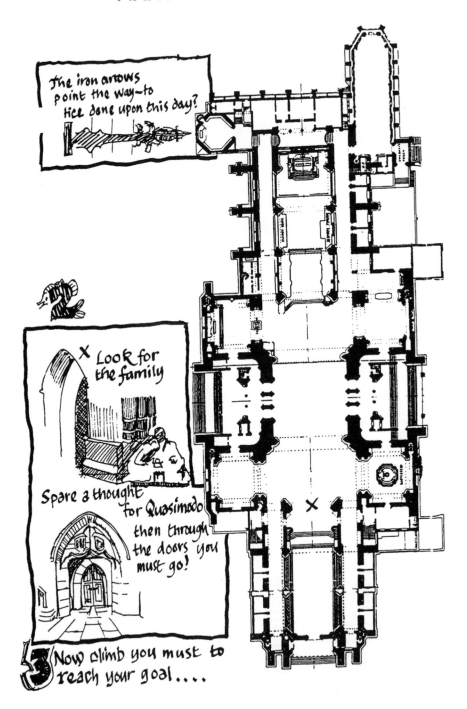

The iron arrows point the way—to tiel done upon this day?

X Look for the family

Spare a thought for Quasimodo then through the doors you must go!

Now climb you must to reach your goal....

QUASIMODO'S MAP OF LIVERPOOL CATHEDRAL.

.... five Arches (counting two as whole)

~~ your quest IS AT AN END!

X You may begin your quest for Quasimodo beneath the ╪ bridge.

Quasimodo has made this plan ⁓

Now, onwards, upwards-find the ropes, on these you may depend ~ seek higher yet and find

Liverpool Cathedral

attempts to communicate with him would fall on his deaf ears, but as he disappeared into the recesses above them, he would throw maps (which he had drawn "freehand") down from the gallery into the void, shouting, "If you want me, come and find me. . . ." They would have to read the clues on the maps to find him (see the illustration on pages 148–149).

The drama would also provide a means of exploring and reflecting on the nature and quality of relationships, the issue of judging people by appearances, and historical and current attitudes toward people with disabilities. The children would have to reach conclusions on characters, their motivations, prejudices, and attitudes. They would also have to read the events that they were witnessing and decide where responsibility lay. We would also make space for them to suggest refinement and changes to what they had seen. The past and present would, within the proposed framework, constantly inform each other.

## 6. Cross-phase Liaison

In the planning, it seemed feasible for schools to work together on the day. This cross-phase liaison between different schools would foster dialogue and networking between teachers and encourage children to work cooperatively with other students. Special needs children would be placed with mainstream groups. Secondary students would work with children from primaries, inner city primaries would accompany suburban schools. Teachers were uncertain about some of the combinations, but we insisted on trusting the power of the drama to divert, alleviate, and surmount potential problems. In all, there would be ten "performances" over two weeks. Twenty schools would be involved, with a total of 40 teachers and 350 students.

## 7. Timing and Administration

The intention was to spend the best part of a day on the drama. The children would arrive at a side entrance just before nine in the morning and be escorted to a large concert room in the crypt. Some schools wanted to dress in costume, and this room afforded them a space to change and to have their sandwiches at lunchtime. It was also the place where we would spend the opening hour preparing students for the day. After this initial hour they would be ready to ascend into the central space, the nave, where the story was about to unfold. For about an hour they would see and take part in the events enacted, and then for the final forty-five minutes of the morning they would return to the chapter house to make judgments about what Quasimodo had done. This was intense activity, but merely traveling around the building and climbing the spiral staircases (720 steps up and 720 steps

AT THE START OF THE DRAMA, THE STUDENTS ARE ESCORTED TO
THE CRYPT.

down) took a great deal of time, and the range of events and locations was so
varied that they hardly had time to settle before things suddenly changed.
The afternoon session lasted for one and a half hours with a similar chrono-
logical breakdown between experience and reflection.

The teachers were given full information about timing, facilities, learning objectives and procedures before the day. Many of the schools involved
did some preparation before the visit, but we still felt that there was a need
for specific guidance on the day. Issues of safety had to be worked through.
We had to talk about sharing the day with other schools and advice had to
be given about ignoring guides and tourists and any other activities going on
within the cathedral's precincts.

## The Drama: Questions Answered

We have referred to many of the incidents that occurred within the drama in
the planning stage, but this is a brief flavor of some of the things that happened on the days themselves. The very first performance was not without
attendant difficulties. The drama had been planned as part of a celebratory
language festival, and there were about two hundred children visiting the
exhibition in the nave as our first company of participants emerged into the

light. In addition, another fifty children were rehearsing a dance performance close to the tower space. The guides and the interpreters were also busy showing people around. Cameras were clicking and all was noise and bustle. It had the makings of a disaster. It occurred to us, however that we might be able to turn this farrago and commotion to our advantage. Over the centuries attitudes toward church have changed considerably. Nowadays a reverential hush tends to pervade churches, but in medieval times they would most likely have been bursting with the activities of buying and selling, to-ing and fro-ing. Unexpectedly we had been presented with a modern parallel to a historical situation. We explained this to the students and, almost paradoxically, when they came into the frenetic space it seemed to help them focus more sharply.

They were duly welcomed by our Archdeacon, who enlisted their help in finding Quasimodo and warned about gypsies, thieves, and cutpurses who were active in the cathedral precincts. As the dancers tumbled and shouted and the festival proceeded hard by it was easy to appreciate that a great metropolitan cathedral was the ideal environment for robbers to ply their nefarious trades.

When Quasimodo had appeared and thrown down his maps, the unexpected occurred. It took well over half a minute for them to descend to the floor. We watched transfixed as the children ran under the drifting papers and tried to predict where they would fall. Suddenly, however, the central space was alive with children, not just of our party, but other visiting students who had deserted the exhibition and run up from the nave to snatch at the paper shower. They were led reluctantly back by their teachers as the Quasimodo party read the clues on the maps.

The group interpreted and followed Quasimodo's instructions and started to climb the spiral staircase. Some concern had been expressed in rehearsal about what would happen as they ascended. Would they be bored? Would the interruption in the action distract them? Would they get too tired?

The concerns proved to be unfounded. The climb actually had very positive effects. Each ascent provided room to think about what had just happened and an opportunity to predict what might happen next. It was absolutely necessary after highly fraught and dramatic moments for the intensity to sink in, and the climbs and descents afforded that necessary space. They talked on the stairs about what they had seen, and if they talked about other things as well it made no difference at all to their involvement in the drama. One does not have to be precious about sustaining a role.

The dark, dusty steps with occasional windows lighting the way enhanced the air of excitement. This was augmented by the candles and the sound of Quasimodo's singing, echoing down the stairs from above. His song

AS QUASIMODO THROWS HIS MAPS FROM THE GALLERY HIGH ABOVE, PUPILS
STRETCH TO CATCH THEM FLUTTERING DOWN.

IN THE CHAPTER HOUSE JEHAN ASKS THE CITIZENS TO DELIBERATE ON WHO
IS RESPONSIBLE FOR THE KIDNAPPING OF ESMERALDA.

sound of Quasimodo's singing, echoing down the stairs from above. His song was the strongest incentive to climb higher.

At one stage, Quasimodo was beaten (out of view) by Frollo and led by the students to be tried in the chapter house. Some of the students seized the opportunity to abuse him even more, but the trial in the chapter house allowed us to challenge historical attitudes toward disabled people and without censure or blame to make the students realize the inappropriateness of their response.

The concerns about heterogeneous groups of students working together proved unfounded, as the need to fathom the plot and determine the guilty and the innocent overcame differences.

## Follow-Up

Back in school we looked at some of the issues that the day had raised. The teachers had been given a pack of ideas and possible areas to explore, but it is a frequent concern that children do not make the connections between the metaphor of drama and their own lives; so where possible, the project actors and teachers worked together on relating what they had seen to the children's personal experience. We also wanted to convince teachers that they could build on the resonances of the drama and integrate drama strategies into their teaching.

The workshop foci were: judging people by their appearances, challenging superficial assessments of people, abuses of power by those in authority, the way that gypsies and transients are treated by the establishment, and the assumptions that are made about the threats they pose to society.

It was remarkable that, even when the workshops took place weeks after the cathedral visit, the resonances of the day were still powerfully and graphically called to mind and reconstructed by the children.

## SPECIAL NEEDS: ACCOMMODATING ALL IN A LOCATION

Special Needs students were very much a part of the proceedings cited above, but in some cases, disability needs to be dealt with specifically and creatively.

On a drama project involving over eighty children and twenty-five teachers from a range of special needs and mainstream schools, the theme of dinosaurs was being pursued. The project was developmental, and the children came together each week for an hour's workshop. We explored archaeological process, reconstructing dinosaurs from their remains, we talked about the way dinosaurs hunted and survived and the possibilities of finding any alive today. The more the sessions progressed and the greater the students' involvement in the subject, the more it became evident that they were desperate to go in search of the creatures themselves. An "expedition" was planned in one of the workshops, and we rehearsed activities like climbing and hacking through jungles, using camouflage netting from a friendly army base. This went well enough, but it soon became apparent that it would be so much more exciting if we could use a location that replicated the real thing.

We planned a mountaineering expedition to the home of the dinosaurs and secured the assistance of a group of experienced mountaineers to lead us up. The climb was not especially difficult, but it looked hard, and the children were roped together as they climbed toward the pterodactyl's lair.

There was one girl called Rosy, however, who was wheelchair bound and we were keen not to exclude her from the activity. It is possible for people to climb within wheelchairs, but this was not feasible on the cliff we had chosen for our expedition. So a parallel narrative was devised to complement the dinosaur and accommodate Rosy. The mountaineers would also be involved on a quest. They would be searching for their lost tribal queen, and our map happened to reveal where she was located as well as the dinosaurs. When we reached the clifftop, Queen Rosy was sitting in her wheelchair outside her tent. She had been driven there beforehand by another route. The tribe were beside themselves with joy as they celebrated being reunited with their monarch.

Later we performed our drama about dinosaurs in one of the school halls, which had been converted into a lost world by the judicious spreading of landscaped canvas floor cloths, leaves, netting, and hanging creepers. Rosy appeared in a wheelchair to which wings had been attached and as the wheels turned the wings flapped majestically and powerfully for all to see.

A similar project was undertaken a year later. This time the expedition element took place in an overgrown quarry. A class of physically disabled students were involved, and it was important that they play as significant a role at the quarry as the able-bodied youngsters. They occupied a hill overlooking the "lost world" and from there, equipped with walkie-talkies, they guided the rest of the party to locations that were not visible at ground level. They also gave instructions to a party of adult helpers about the design and layout of their base camp and constructed a cage in which any captured specimens could be kept while the whole group deliberated whether they should be killed or taken to a zoo and studied back home or released back into the wild.

Their role was crucial to the success of the enterprise and their contribution underlined the important of communication and the value of team work.

# Epilogue

The preceding pages will, we hope, have given you a flavor of the possibilities Drama offers. Our experiences in teaching continue to emphasize its value, potential and unrivaled dynamic for promoting learning.

The teacher of a class of sixteen-year-olds who are about to leave school is about to take a lesson on interview skills. They are, in her own words, lethargic and down. The discussion drifts without focus or conviction. The recalcitrant class voices its frustration. "Why should we?" "What's in it for us?" "It's boring."

To be honest, they're right. It's time for the injection of a new stimulus, a fresh angle and approach. The teacher dons a T-shirt over her smart suit. "Life's A Beach" it proclaims. "All right. I'm Samantha Lobb (S. Lobb). My mates call me Sammy. I'm dead bored and I've got a motto. Wanna hear it? [Nods]—'Why should I?' "

They warm to her. The tempo has changed. The atmosphere is more relaxed but also more focused. Around that pivotal moment different realities revolve and coexist: the reality of their teacher with her school wear still clearly visible beneath her T-shirt playing someone else; the reality of her relating to their language and perceptions, breaking down barriers and inviting their participation; the reality of a character who reflects their experience, and with the very perceptions and attributes they themselves had come up with moments before; the reality of a vivid and relevant three-dimensional image set up in their presence, born of a discussion that had length and breadth but no depth of feeling and engagement. All these realities are encapsulated in that simple moment.

"I'm looking for a job. My mum's ill, my sister can't work anymore. Her kid's ill and I need the money to keep us all together. So I'm just off to the Job Center. Hey, you don't know what it's like in there, do you? You do! You couldn't tell us, could you? I feel a bit nervous, like, you know how it is. . . ."

CHILDREN INTERACT WITH THEATRE IN EDUCATION ACTORS.

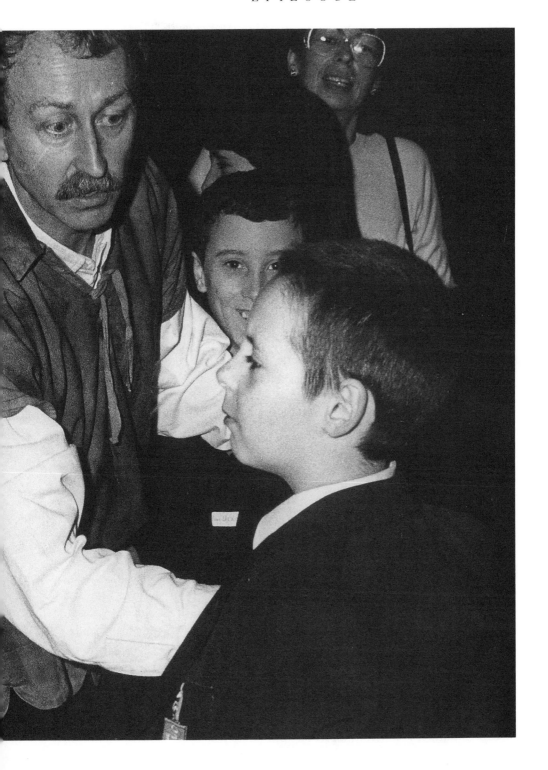

They suggest the scene. The tables, the chairs, the personnel, the other people in the room, their thoughts, their hopes, their fears. The students write job ads for the display boards. They buzz. They want to know what will become of this person. They want to know what will happen in the office they have created, in the play they have cast, and the text they are about to construct.

What had created the turnaround in attitude? What's going on now that wasn't happening before? It isn't easy to sum it up simply, but if we were to confine ourselves to one word it would surely be recognition— a recognition that creates ripple upon ripple of meaning for the participants.

A student volunteers to be a member of the staff at the Job Center and sits behind a desk. Sammy turns to her. "Hey, girl, these 'ere cards, do I have to bring them over there or what?"

Laughter all round but this is too serious to be mere humor. It is laughter born of recognition—recognition of people and situation. They may not have been here specifically, to this particular place, but as they hear and see Sammy they know about not knowing what to say next, about getting the tone of voice wrong, about being so embarrassed that the only sound that emerges is aggressive and defensive at the same time; and as they look at the woman behind the desk they recognize the frustration that deliverers of the unpalatable have felt throughout history when people air their feelings and make their complaints known.

So we set up the image together and together we create a dynamic that can resonate not just for the present but as a window into the past or a vision of the future. The ripples eddy into questions: Why does this happen? Who is responsible? Where does Sammy go from here? What would *you* do? What can *we* do? Can it be otherwise? How might it look? How could it be better? What can we learn from this? What other situations might our learning apply to?

This isn't just the Art of Drama, though Art it clearly is, with its elements of tension, reversal, character, motivation, engagement, humor, and tragedy, but the Art of Learning as well. It is a way of learning that we can enter into, not as passive audiences, mere recipients of someone else's ideas, words, and thoughts, but as active players in our own versions of texts that we create, refine, adapt, and change together.

In truth, this medium of Drama, this basic to which everyone relates, should occupy the educational center stage, and not wait hopefully in the wings for other curricular leading lights to fail. It should be encouraged by its adherents and its occasional acolytes to seize its moment and fulfill its potential, for it holds the key to the greatest power we know, the power to unlock our imaginations and share its wealth with our fellows. It is time to act.

# Select Bibliography

Allen, John. 1979. *Drama in Schools: Its Theory and Practice.* Heinemann.

Barker, Clive. 1977. *Theatre Games.* Methuen.

Barker, Howard. 1993. *Arguments for a Theatre.* 2nd ed. Manchester University Press.

Barton, John. 1984. *Playing Shakespeare.* Methuen.

Bennet, Stuart. 1984. *Drama: The Practice of Freedom.* National Association for the Teaching of Drama paper.

Berry, Cecily. 1987. *The Actor and His Text.* Virgin Books.

Boal, Augusto. 1979. *Theatre of the Oppressed.* Pluto.

———. 1992. *Games for Actors and Non-Actors.* Routledge.

Bolton, Gavin. 1979. *Towards a Theory of Drama in Education.* Longman.

———. 1984. *Drama as Education.* Longman.

———. 1992. *New Perspectives on Classroom Drama,* Simon and Schuster.

Brook, Peter. 1968. *The Empty Space.* Penguin.

———. 1988. *The Shifting Point.* Methuen.

Bristol, Michael. 1992. *Carnival and Theatre: Plebeian Culture and the Structure of Authority in Renaissance England.* Routledge.

Bruner, Jerome. 1971. *Towards a Theory of Instruction.* Harvard University Press.

Byron, Ken. "Drama at the Crossroads" *2D.* Autumn 1986, Vol. 6, No. 1, and Autumn 1987, Vol. 7, No. 1.

———. 1986. *Drama in the English Classroom.* Methuen.

———. (Editor) 1989, October. *The Fight for Drama—The Fight for Education: Keynote Speeches by Edward Bond and Dorothy Heathcote.* National Association for the Teaching of Drama Conference.

Craig, Sandy. 1980. *Dreams and Deconstructions: Alternative Theatre in Britain.* Amber Lane Press.

Davies, Geoff. 1983. *Practical Primary Drama.* Heinemann.

Davis, David, and Lawrence, Chris (Editors). 1986. *Gavin Bolton: Selected Writings.* Longman.

Day, Christopher and Norman, John (Editors). 1983. *Issues in Educational Drama.* The Falmer Press.

Dobson, Warwick (Editor). 1982. *Bolton at the Barbican.* National Association for the Teaching of Drama paper.

Dodgson, Elyse. 1984. *Motherland.* Heinemann.

England, Alan. 1990. *Theatre for the Young.* Macmillan.

Ewards, Derek and Mercer, Neil. 1987. *Common Knowledge: The Development of Understanding in the Classroom.* Routledge.

Fines, John, and Verrier, Ralph. 1974. *The Drama of History.* New University Education.

Fleming, Michael. 1994. *Starting Drama Teaching.* David Fulton Publishers.

Frost, Anthony, and Yarrow, Ralph. 1990. *Improvisation in Drama.* Macmillan.

Gardner, Howard. 1991. *The Unschooled Mind: How Children Think and How Schools Should Teach.* Fontana Press.

Gaskill, William. 1988. *A Sense of Direction.* Faber and Faber.

Goode, Tony (Editor). 1984. *Heathcote at the National: Drama Teacher—Facilitator or Manipulator?* National Association for the Teaching of Drama paper.

Heathcote, Dorothy. 1980. *Drama as Context.* National Association for the Teaching of English paper.

Heathcote, Dorothy, and Bolton, Gavin. 1995. *Drama for Learning: Dorothy Heathcote's Mantle of the Expert Approach to Education.* Heinemann.

Hemming, James. 1985. *Drama and the Politics of Ignorance.* National Association for the Teaching of Drama paper.

Hornbrook, David. 1989. *Education and Dramatic Art.* Blackwell Education.

———. 1991. *Education in Drama: Casting the Dramatic Curriculum.* Falmer Press.

Hutchcroft, Diana. 1981. *Making Language Work.* McGraw-Hill Company (UK) Ltd.

Innes, Christopher. 1993. *Avant Garde Theatre 1892–1992.* Routledge.

Jackson, Tony (Editor). 1980. *Learning Through Theatre: Essays and Casebooks on Theatre in Education.* Manchester University Press. 1993. Second edition, updated and revised as *Learning Through Theatre: New Perspectives on Theatre in Education.* Routledge.

Jeffcoate, Robert. 1992. *Starting English Teaching.* Routledge.

Johnson, Liz and O'Neill, Cecily. 1984. *Dorothy Heathcote: Collected Writings on Drama and Education.* Hutchinson.

Johnstone, Keith. 1981. *Impro.* Methuen.

Kershaw, Baz. 1992. *The Politics of Performance: Radical Theatre as Cultural Intervention.* Routledge.

Lawrence, Chris (Editor). 1993. *Voices for Change.* National Drama publication.

Linnell, Rosemary. 1982. *Approaching Classroom Drama.* Arnold.

McGrath, John. 1981. *A Good Night Out: Popular Theatre: Audience, Class, and Form.* Methuen.

————. 1990. *The Bone Won't Break: On Theatre and Hope in Hard Times.* Methuen.

McGregor, Lynn; Tate, Maggie; and Robinson, Ken. 1977. *Learning Through Drama.* Heinemann.

Morgan, Norah and Saxton, Juliana. 1987. *Teaching Drama: A Mind of Many Wonders.* Hutchinson.

Neelands, Jonothan. 1984. *Making Sense of Drama: A Guide to Classroom Practice.* Heinemann.

————. 1990. *Structuring Drama Work.* Edited Goode, T. Cambridge University Press.

Nixon, Jon. 1982. *Drama and the Whole Curriculum.* Hutchinson.

Norman, John. 1981. *Drama in Education: A Curriculum for Change.* National Association for the Teaching of Drama Conference Report. Kemble Press.

O'Neill, Cecily; Lambert, Alan; Linnell, Rosemary; and Warr-Wood, Janet. 1976. *Drama Guidelines.* Heinemann.

O'Neill, Cecily and Lambert, Alan. 1982. *Drama Structures: A Practical Handbook for Teachers.* Hutchinson.

O'Toole, John. 1976. *Theatre in Education: New Objectives for Theatre—New Techniques in Education.* Hodder and Stoughton.

O'Toole, John, and Haseman, Brad. 1987. *Dramawise—An Introduction to GCSE Drama.* Heinemann.

O'Toole, John. 1992. *The Process of Drama: Negotiating Art and Meaning.* Routledge.

Richardson, Robin. 1990. *Daring to be a Teacher.* Trentham Books.

Robinson, Ken (Editor). 1980. *Exploring Theatre and Education.* Heinemann.

Rodenburg, Patsy. 1993. *The Right to Speak: Working with the Voice.* Routledge.

————. 1994. *The Need for Words: Voice and Text.* Routledge.

Schutzman, Mady and Cohen-Cruz, Jan. 1994. *Playing Boal: Theatre, Therapy, Activism.* Routledge.

Slade, Peter. 1954. *Child Drama.* University of London Press.

Spolin, Viola. 1963. *Improvisation for the Theatre.* Northwestern University Press.

Stabler, Tom. 1979. *Drama in Primary Schools.* Macmillan.

Vygotsky, Lev. 1978. *Mind in Society: The Development of Higher Psychological Processes.* Harvard University Press.

Wagner, Betty Jane. 1979. *Dorothy Heathcote: Drama as a Learning Medium.* Hutchinson.

Watkins, Brian. 1981. *Drama and Education.* Batsford.

Way, Brian. 1967. *Development Through Drama.* Longman.

Williams, Raymond. 1983. *Writing in Society.* Vero.

Woolland, Brian. 1993. *The Teaching of Drama in the Primary School.* Longman.

Wootton, Margaret. 1982. *New Directions in Drama Teaching: Studies in Secondary School Practice.* Heinemann.